Student Mobility and the Internationalization of Higher Education:

National Policies and Strategies from Six World Regions

A *Project Atlas*® Report

Student Mobility and the Internationalization of Higher Education:

National Policies and Strategies from Six World Regions

A *Project Atlas*® Report

Edited by Rajika Bhandari, Raisa Belyavina and Robert Gutierrez

INSTITUTE OF INTERNATIONAL EDUCATION

New York, NY

Compiled and published by the Institute of International Education
with contributions from *Project Atlas*® partner organizations.

IIE publications can be purchased at: www.iiebooks.org

The Institute of International Education
809 United Nations Plaza, New York, NY 10017

© 2011 by the Institute of International Education
All rights reserved. Published 2011
Printed in the United States of America
ISBN-13: 978-0-87206-341-9
ISBN-10: 0-87206-341-0

Library of Congress Cataloging-in-Publication Data

Student mobility and the internationalization of higher education : national policies and strategies from six world regions / edited by Rajika Bhandari, Raisa
Belyavina, and Robert Gutierrez.
       p. cm.
  Includes bibliographical references.
  ISBN 978-0-87206-341-9 (pbk.)
  1. Students, Foreign--Cross-cultural studies. 2. Student mobility--Cross-cultural
studies. 3. Education and globalization--Cross-cultural studies. 4. Higher education and state--Cross-cultural studies. I. Bhandari, Rajika. II. Belyavina, Raisa. III.
Gutierrez, Robert.
  LB2375.S745 2011
  378.1'982691--dc22
                              2011000484

TABLE OF CONTENTS

FIGURES

National Strategies and Global Student Mobility: An Introduction[1]

By Rajika Bhandari, Institute of International Education (IIE)

Global higher education mobility is a rapidly growing phenomenon affecting the management of resources and students among institutions and nations worldwide. Since 2000, the number of students traveling to another country in pursuit of higher education increased by 65 percent, totaling some 3.3 million students globally. Although the rapid growth of mobility is relatively recent, the desire to acquire a higher education beyond national borders is itself not new; students and scholars have always sought learning at the best higher education institutions around the world as a way to broaden their educational and cultural horizons. What has changed, however, is the overall context of global mobility, both in terms of who is going where, and the mix of host and sending countries. As nations and world economies continue to address migration through a variety of mechanisms—from constricting or loosening entry policies to providing incentives for skilled migration and talent—these decisions tend to drive global migration patterns of students as much as "immigrants" in the traditional sense.

While Anglophone and Western European countries such as the United States, United Kingdom, Australia, France, and Germany have historically attracted the largest number of international students, other countries have boosted their internationalization strategies in recent years to attract more students, build university linkages, and develop joint research programs. Most countries now view international academic mobility and educational

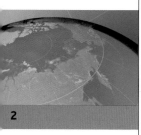

exchanges as critical components for sharing knowledge, building intellectual capital and remaining competitive in a globalizing world. It is also a way to foster mutual understanding and cooperation, especially in a climate of increased diplomacy and security.

For the suppliers of international education—namely host countries and institutions—there are a variety of objectives and approaches to engaging in academic exchange, and those that are most effective in internationalizing are characterized by flexibility and a willingness to adapt to new realities in the complex world of higher education. Common to the best of them are certain elements such as commitment to academic excellence, to fair and open access for candidates, and to a diverse range of participants. Most also face similar challenges, such as how to cope with rapidly expanding opportunities and interest in study abroad with limited or shrinking resources.

The current report sets out to capture the dynamic role of key host and sending countries that are engaged in academic mobility, taking a close look at the national-level plans and strategies that many have developed to attract more international students to their shores and to encourage more of their own students to go overseas. In doing so, the report draws upon the members of *Project Atlas* ®, a unique and global community of academic mobility researchers that represent 21 national-level governmental, non-governmental, and international organizations engaged in international educational exchange and researchers with an interest in sharing harmonized and current data on student mobility. Initiated in 2001 with support from the Ford Foundation and currently supported by the U.S. Department of State and the participating members in other countries, *Project Atlas* and its associated web portal, the *Atlas of Student Mobility (www.iie.org/projectatlas),* provide a comprehensive global picture of international student mobility for more than 17 leading destination countries.

This introduction to the report provides an overview of *Project Atlas*, the changing landscape of international education hosting and sending countries, and the internationalization strategies in place to attract more international students.

Project Atlas: A Shared Framework for Student Mobility Data

The foundations for *Project Atlas* were established in May 2001 at a meeting in France that was attended by representatives from key national bodies and non-governmental organizations involved in international educational exchanges and mobility who had expressed an interest in developing an effective approach to a common data set for global mobility. Representatives from the Organization for Economic Co-operation and Development (OECD) and the United Nations Educational, Scientific and Cultural Organization (UNESCO), agencies that are mandated to collect global mobility data, also participated. By creating a shared framework for measuring and understanding international mobility, the goal was to highlight the truly global aspects of higher education, make apparent the emerging world higher education economy, and establish a conversation space for those concerned with global education mobility issues.

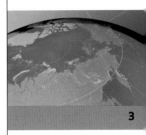

3

To begin with, the group encountered a number of challenges inherent in the field of global student mobility: how do we find a common definition of an international student and how do we measure the movements of students around the world? Despite varied national data collection strategies and time-tables, can we develop a framework for sharing data that is timely and accessible to researchers around the globe? While the field of academic migration was vast and complex, our ability to document and understand student mobility from a global perspective had not kept pace with the growth in numbers and variety of international study experiences. Reliable and consistent data was needed to respond effectively to global developments in higher education. Yet there was surprisingly limited data available to countries on which they could base their decision-making or frame their policy discussion. Even though many countries have national data collection organizations, the resulting data vary widely from country-to-country in timeliness, data definitions, and scope. The variation in national degree and qualifications structures across countries also makes comparative analysis difficult. What was needed was a global and consistent source of baseline data as well as a forum within which national efforts could be compared and benchmarked.

It was this gap in the mobility field that *Project Atlas* attempted to fill. The group agreed that the first requirement was to establish mechanisms that

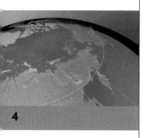

would better and consistently describe international student mobility through the compilation and aggregation of data available to national agencies and related organizations, followed by wide dissemination of findings. A first step in this direction was the formulation of the following standard definition of mobile students that all *Project Atlas* partners would adhere to when sharing data: *Students who undertake all or part of their higher education experience in a country other than their home country* OR *students who travel across a national boundary to a country other than their home country to undertake all or part of their higher education experience.* It was envisioned that this broad conceptual definition could then be implemented on a country- or region-specific basis. The Institute of International Education (IIE) also published a seminal book in 2003, bringing together international mobility data from 21 major host countries. This *Atlas of Student Mobility* graphically presented the data in various ways, including analysis by sending countries and in comparison with other relevant data. Disseminated widely in the U.S. and overseas, this initial publication's purpose was to enable the reader to view the emerging global higher education space as a whole—as more than just the sum of its national host country parts.

Project Atlas Today

Over the next decade, *Project Atlas* expanded its membership to include established and emerging host countries located in both the developed and developing world. To increase access to users worldwide, all data gathered through the project was moved online and continues to be disseminated through the *Atlas of Student Mobility* web portal. With the goal of highlighting national policies that facilitate global mobility, Atlas partner organizations use the project website to share the strategies and initiatives their countries and governments have undertaken to increase international educational exchange. For instance, *Project Atlas* tells us how China has moved from being the leading sending country for international students to now also being one of the top ten host countries, and how South Africa is growing as a regional host for students throughout Africa and beyond. To capture more fully the increasingly important role that newer "host" countries are now playing in global mobility, an ongoing priority for the project is to identify and involve more partners from Asia, Latin America, the Middle East, and Africa. Currently, there are 21 project partners comprising 17 countries and four research affiliates, representing six world regions.

Project Atlas Country Partners, 2010

Association of Indian Universities (AIU)
Australian Education International (AEI)
British Council
Canadian Bureau for International Education (CBIE)
CampusFrance
Centre for International Mobility (CIMO), Finland
China Scholarship Council (CSC)
Education Ireland
Fundación Universidad.es, Spain
German Academic Exchange Service (DAAD)
Institute of International Education (IIE), USA
International Education Association of South Africa (IEASA)
Japan Student Services Organization (JASSO)
National Association of Universities and Higher Education Institutions (ANUIES), Mexico
Netherlands Organization for International Cooperation in Higher Education (NUFFIC)
New Zealand Ministry of Education
Swedish Institute

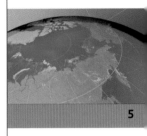

Project Atlas Research Affiliates, 2010

Center for International Higher Education (CIHE), Boston College
International Association of Universities (IAU)
Organisation for Economic Co-operation and Development (OECD)
UNESCO Institute for Statistics (UIS)

The Project's regularly updated website makes the data available to a wider audience and provides an online forum for project partners. The group also meets at least once a year to engage in ongoing dialogue and cooperation. These collaborative meetings not only assist partners in developing joint data collection standards and practices, but also strengthen collaboration and shrink the "competitive" prism through which international student mobility discussions are often viewed. Between 2004 and 2010, IIE has co-hosted international student mobility conferences and _Project Atlas_-related meetings with _Project Atlas_ partner organizations in the U.S., China, Mexico, the UK, India, the Netherlands, Kenya, and Spain. In addition to sharing mobility data, these meetings provide partners an opportunity to jointly develop research activities on topics such as cross-border education, student-level attitudinal surveys, and longitudinal trends in mobility for certain key host

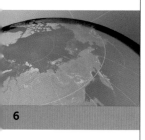

countries. A more recent goal of the Project has been to engage in capacity-building activities for less-experienced emerging destinations to design and implement a system to collect mobility data. Along these lines, IIE collaborated with the African Network for Internationalization of Education (ANIE) in September 2009 to hold a two-day capacity building workshop in Kenya on global student migration and best practices in collecting data on higher education migration.

The Expanding Pie of Global Student Mobility: Traditional Hosts and New Players

Developed countries in Europe, North America, and Oceania have dominated the global mobility landscape, with Europe serving as the top destination until World War II and the U.S. taking over as the top host from the 1950s onwards. In 2009, six countries hosted over 60 percent of the world's tertiary-level mobile students: the U.S. (20 percent), the UK (13 percent), France (eight percent), Australia, Germany and China (seven percent each). The U.S. continues to host the largest number and proportion of international students pursuing a higher education outside of their home country (690,923 students in 2009/10, followed by the UK at 415,585 students in 2009). The shift in the U.S. world share as a host of international students from 28 percent to 20 percent over the past decade is due to multiple factors, including the increased capacity of the higher education sector in many non-traditional destinations, especially in Asia, to host domestic as well as international students; strong national-level internationalization policies and strategies in competing destinations; domestic economic, demographic, and workforce conditions that might affect students' decisions regarding an overseas education; and the rise of non-traditional forms of educational delivery such as virtual learning and offshore education.

The movement of students has primarily been from developing to developed countries and while this overall trend continues today, the situation is changing, with interesting variations emerging in which several unexpected players are now engaged in what might best be described as a "global competition" for international students. The overall pie of global mobility is expanding with more countries emerging as important destinations for international students. Newer host countries such as China are seeing rapid increases in the numbers of international students. Several other countries in the Asia Pacific region—Japan, Malaysia, New Zealand, Singapore,

South Korea, and Thailand—have stepped up their efforts to internationalize and to attract more international students. While this has resulted in a somewhat smaller market share for top host countries, it is nonetheless a positive development as it has brought more countries into the field of international education and has changed the relationship between sending and receiving countries from a unidirectional "brain drain" type of mobility to one of dynamic, mutual exchange.

Several traditional host countries, along with newer players in Asia and Europe, have allocated tens of millions of dollars to launch large-scale initiatives over the past few years. Government-supported efforts by key host countries, including nationally coordinated campaigns by the UK, Australia, Germany, France, New Zealand and others, feature sophisticated marketing strategies.

Launched in 1998, the UK's £5 million "Prime Minister's Initiative" was one of the earliest and was updated in 2000 as the "Education UK" brand, a coordinated approach to marketing British institutions abroad that is available for use by any UK campus. Other recent UK initiatives include the Science and Engineering Graduate Scheme (2004), the UK-China Higher Education Program (2005), and the UK-India Education and Research Initiative (2006). These and other key efforts, described in greater detail in this report, are proving very persuasive, especially in recruiting self-funded students from some of the large sending countries in Asia.

Many traditional hosts are also formalizing the link between higher education and the skilled job market by implementing policies that encourage international graduates to enter the workforce of the host country, especially in scientific and technical fields. Scotland announced a "Post-Study Worker Scheme" aimed at attracting 8,000 foreign professionals per year up until 2009 by allowing international students who graduate from a Scottish university to remain for two years of post-graduation employment. Supplementing efforts by individual host countries in Europe, the European Union (EU) has also launched initiatives to recruit science and technology researchers from around the world in an attempt to compete with America's well-funded research universities and laboratories that reputedly attract the world's best and brightest science and technology (S&T) talent. The U.S., too, has expanded employment options for graduating foreign students in the

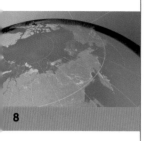

sciences and engineering by extending the length of the Optional Practical Training (OPT) program from its original 12 months to 29 months for science and technology fields, although it remains to be seen whether employers will be able to provide such opportunities in the current weak job market.

At the other end of the spectrum, countries that were primarily "sending" countries have now also developed their own internationalization strategies to attract foreign students and encourage international educational exchange. This new era of internationalization is most evident in Asia. Singapore has been making strides in this area with the establishment of Education Singapore, a new agency charged with promoting and marketing Singapore abroad and with attracting 150,000 foreign students by 2015. Malaysia seeks to attract 80,000 international students by 2010; China seeks to host 500,000 by 2020; and Japan has set the goal of hosting 300,000 international students by 2020.

These positive developments notwithstanding, developing countries have traditionally been the "suppliers" of international students but now face interesting challenges as they are poised to also become popular study destinations. They are likely to face the dilemma of how to increase the capacity of their higher education systems to provide adequate opportunities for their expanding college-age population while also accommodating incoming international students and engaging in the type of international educational exchange that is necessary in today's globally competitive world. Last but not least, a related challenge for developing countries hoping to attract back their internationally trained nationals will be to ensure adequate employment opportunities and an appropriate standard of living so that the home country also benefits from this globally mobile talent pool.

Overview of Report

Against the backdrop of student mobility trends, this report provides a broad view of what 17 key countries are doing at the national and institutional level to attract international students and to send more of their students abroad. The focus is not on the mobility data itself, but rather on the context—the internationalization policies and strategies that ultimately drive mobility numbers for each host and sending country. Each of the country sections in the report is authored by a *Project Atlas* partner, reflecting their in-depth knowledge of that country's internationalization strategies. The report concludes with a comprehensive look at the internationalization efforts of various countries and higher education systems, as documented by the 3rd Global Survey on Internationalization of Higher Education, conducted by the International Association of Universities (IAU), based in Paris. The findings of the survey—which serves as a periodic "report card" on internationalization efforts worldwide—are a reminder that even though significant strides have been made in making higher education internationalization (and student mobility as a key component of it) a national-level priority, there is much that remains to be done to ensure full implementation of national and institutional policies and goals.

[1] Part of this introduction appears in Bhandari, R. and Peggy Blumenthal, *International Students and Global Mobility in Higher Education: National Trends and New Directions*, 2010, Palgrave Macmillan, and is reproduced here with the permission of Palgrave Macmillan.

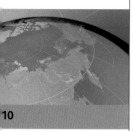

10

REGION: **Sub-Saharan Africa**

Africans studying outside of their home country comprise ten percent of international students in the world (OECD, 2008). UNESCO reports that sub-Saharan Africa has the highest outbound student mobility rate (the number of students studying outside of their home country) in the world. Nearly six percent of all sub-Saharan African students study overseas, a rate three times higher than the global average. In many African countries, a majority of students interested in pursuing higher education leave the region to do so rather than continuing their higher education domestically. This leaves sub-Saharan Africa drained of its most valuable resource: its educated youth. In many countries, there is limited capacity in the tertiary education sphere to accommodate all students who wish to pursue higher education in their home country. The issue of quality also plays a role in why students choose to leave their home country (and often the continent) in pursuit of higher education. Countries in which more than 40 percent of students study abroad include: Cape Verde (outbound mobility ratio of 92 percent), Swaziland (52 percent), Botswana (50 percent), Lesoto (45 percent) and Namibia (42 percent). South Africa, Democratic Republic of the Congo and Ethiopia have the lowest outbound ratios, ranging from 0.7 percent to 1.5 percent (UNESCO, 2010).

The number of students studying in Africa from outside of the region is much more limited. Among African countries, South Africa is the leading host destination, with approximately 60,000 international students enrolled in public universities. Over 60 percent of the international students studying in South Africa come from neighboring countries, primarily from Namibia and Zimbabwe. While the number of non-African students studying in Africa has increased steadily in recent years, prospective students still see African higher education institutions as less internationalized than in other world regions, and those who do come to study in Africa usually pursue short-term exchange or study abroad programs.

The major challenge for higher education in Africa is addressing the growing local demand for tertiary education. The need for higher education in sub-Saharan Africa is increasing at the fastest rate in the world and enrollment rates are expected to double every five years (Kishun, 2008). As more African students seek educational opportunities, African education will face tremendous pressure to grow. In the coming years, it is expected that more women will enter the higher education sphere in Africa and addressing issues of gender and economic equity will become a top priority.

As of now, the expansion of higher education in Africa is slow, particularly in the public sector. Historically, the development of the education sector has relied heavily on external assistance, including international aid. With the General Agreement on Trade in Services (GATS) in place, there has been an international shift away from development aid to trade in services, including education. Additionally, the strong push for universal primary education in Africa has redirected donor and state funding away from higher education—even though growing participation in primary and secondary school has spurred the need to expand the tertiary education sector. The major challenge in higher education today is the lack of funding on many levels: international, national, institutional, and individual.

With public universities stretched beyond their capacity to accommodate more students, the private sector for higher education has made significant inroads in the region. The expanding market of private institutions provides more educational opportunities for those who can afford them, but also aggravates the longstanding inequities in the education system, as well as raising issues of quality assurance. Most private higher education providers in sub-Saharan Africa are local, and the region is lagging in the global trend of establishing inter-regional schemes and cross-national educational ventures. There have been efforts to overcome this and a number of international partnerships are being forged as African universities partner with institutions around the world to upgrade and internationalize local universities.[1] As in other regions, a major focus for public and private higher education institutions is to expand access to quality education and to prepare graduates for 21st century careers that meet the workforce needs of the home country.[2]

[1] One example is the creation of international programs aimed to attract students in the region and internationally, such as the University of Nairobi Master's Degree in Education and Emergencies, which will open its doors in Fall 2011. (http://www.theirc.org/news/new-university-ngo-partnership-create-center-excellence-education-emergencies-east-africa-media). Another example is the African Network for Internationalizing Education (ANIE), which aims to advance research, build capacity, and form partnerships to internationalize higher education in Africa (www.anienetwork.org).

[2] For more information on Africa, please see O'Hara, Sabine. (2010). *Higher Education in Africa: Equity, Access, Opportunity*. New York: Institute of International Education.

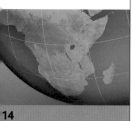

14

By the International Education Association of South Africa (IEASA)

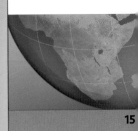

Understanding the current landscape of higher education in Africa provides important context for the discussion of the higher education sector in South Africa and particularly where internationalization efforts fit into the greater picture. The approximately 4.5 million students enrolled in higher education institutions in sub-Saharan Africa represent a mere two percent of the college-aged population. The low enrollment ratio also reflects the small number of institutions and seats available throughout Africa, as most institutions tend to be centralized in major urban areas.

There are a number of structural and demographic challenges facing higher education in Africa. There is increased demand for access to higher education and a general lack of resources in systems that still struggle to overcome colonial impacts. The ever-increasing digital divide presents distinct issues in preparing students for the workforce. An imbalance of graduates in humanities, sciences, and in engineering and technology, leads to poor doctoral output in the high demand areas of biotechnology, information and communications technology, and materials development. Furthermore, attempts to rapidly increase higher education access to keep up with demand have resulted in uneven quality in educational offerings. Gender and class inequities as well as the exorbitant HIV-prevalence rate among 19-24 year olds, particularly in the Sub-Saharan region, present a unique set of challenges to the work of improving capacity and quality in Africa's higher education systems.

South Africa's higher education sector has been in flux for more than a decade, primarily to repair the inequitable access to higher education that

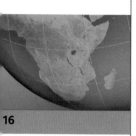

16

was embedded by the apartheid system prior to 1994. The newly elected democratic government implemented drastic measures to rapidly reform the sector, noting the backdrop of the African higher education landscape. Among these was the merger of institutions to achieve a balance in the racial divide, often merging historically black and historically white institutions in an effort to fuse curricula, resources and infrastructure to create a more equitable system. This has been effective in some instances and increased academic access for black South Africans. Despite this larger progress, some higher education institutions continue to struggle with diversity challenges.

Sub-Saharan Africa has one of the highest outbound student mobility rates in the world, with one in 16 students studying outside the borders of their own country. South Africa is also an important hub for African student mobility. The largest senders of international students to South Africa are countries in the Southern African region, followed by students from countries in other parts of Africa. More availability of short-term and exchange programs is attracting growing numbers of students from Europe, Latin America, North America, and Oceania. The country's setting and leading role in Africa, its strong research universities and its relatively advanced stage of development make it an ideal base for studies aimed at understanding the challenges of developing countries in Africa.

International Students at South African Public Higher Education Institutions, Selected Years, 1994-2009

Home Region	1994	1997	2000	2003	2006	2009
Southern African Development Community[1]	6,209	7,822	21,318	36,207	35,917	41,906
Africa (Non-Southern African Development Community)[2]	1,521	2,079	4,263	6,664	8,569	10,663
Non-Africa[3]	4,827	5,268	5,568	7,108	7,673	7,011
No Information on Student Place of Origin			14,228	1,447	1,574	1,276
Total: International Students	12,557	15,169	45,377	51,426	53,733	60,856
Total: South African Students			545,784	666,367	687,650	776,923
Total: Percent International Students in Higher Education			7.68	7.16	7.25	7.26

(Source: South Africa Department of Education, Higher Education Management Information System (HEMIS) Data, September, 2010; Compiled by IEASA.)

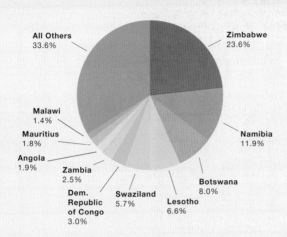

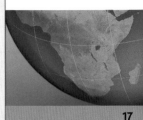

REGION:
Sub-Saharan Africa
COUNTRY:
South Africa

Figure 1: Places of Origin of International Students in South Africa, 2008

Source: IEASA

There has been consistent annual growth in the enrollment of international students at public higher education institutions in South Africa. The domestic growth at tertiary institutions has increased by five percent, while the international student growth rate is ten percent. Given the political and economic turbulence in neighboring Zimbabwe, over twenty percent growth was seen in 2008. It is expected that the number of international students studying in South Africa will continue to increase in the coming years. Study abroad programs are becoming very popular as the world seeks to find out more about South Africa. With South Africa's successful hosting of the World Cup Soccer games in 2010, South Africa is likely to receive more attention in many sectors, including higher education.

Despite the growth in international student enrollments, the number of students enrolled in public universities in South Africa does not represent the full picture of the internationalization of South African institutions. Data on international student enrollment in private institutions is not collected primarily because private higher education institutions are not mandated by the government to keep these records and are not recognized by the government as universities.[4]

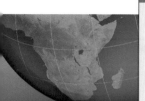

■ The number of international students studying in South Africa has grown dramatically since 1994, from 12,000 to over 60,000 international public university students in 2009, which represents nearly eight percent of the total 800,000 student in South Africa's 23 public universities.

■ The top five places of origin in 2008 were Zimbabwe, Namibia, Botswana, Lesotho and Swaziland.

■ South Africa has become the most popular place to study in Africa and is one of the world's top 20 host destinations for students from the U.S.

■ According to the OECD, South Africa ranks 11th in the world as a destination for international students.

Sources: IEASA, OECD

18

REGION:
Sub-Saharan Africa
COUNTRY:
South Africa

Government efforts to internationalize include a restructuring of South African higher education under new leadership: there are now two ministries, the Department of Higher Education and Training (DHET) and the Department of Basic Education (DBE), focusing on primary and secondary education. Since the split, the Chief Director of International Relations at the DHET has met with the International Education Association of South Africa (IEASA) and each university's international portfolio representatives to better engage the DHET and the department. This engagement signals a positive interest to respond to this growing sector.

The Department of Home Affairs has embarked on an improvement scheme to facilitate inbound student mobility; however, the application process for study visas, postdoctoral fellows, researchers and visitors permits to facilitate an engagement with the higher education sector, could be onerous. The new leadership at the Department is also developing a closer working relationship with IEASA, signaling new support of the concept of internationalization at home. In the hope of bringing the world closer to South Africa, the challenge is still for the department to deliver efficient and equitable service in and out of South Africa. IEASA hopes that a close working relationship will assist in long-term solutions.

The *International Education Association of South Africa (IEASA)* is a non-profit organization established as a result of the need for universities and universities of technology in South Africa to respond to international educational trends. If South Africa is to remain competitive within the global economic environment, it is important that its higher education system provides opportunities for students to obtain a global perspective on their studies. IEASA has been promoting the concept of internationalization since its founding in 1997. The organization promotes internationalization and represents the higher education sector in South Africa to the rest of the world. In this capacity, IEASA establishes international contacts for relationship building that will ultimately benefit students and tertiary institutions and will assist South Africa to be a competitor and participant in world markets.

IEASA releases an annual publication, "Study South Africa," which chronicles the profile of each South African university. Historically, only public South African higher education institutions were allowed to be called universities in South Africa. The 2010 edition profiles the history of the publication and includes information on the expansion of internationalization in higher education in South Africa. It is the only publication that positions South African universities within the international arena. Readership includes international libraries, South African embassies, international funding agencies, international research agencies, local and international governments, study abroad agencies and universities, sister international associations including Asia Pacific Association for International Education (APAIE), European Association for International Education (EAIE) and NAFSA: Association of International Educators, member institution communities and IEASA members. On a policy level, IEASA takes a pro-active role in policy-making; maintains on-going communication and cooperative relationships with government departments and appropriate statutory and other bodies with a view to participating in policy-making on international education. IEASA also monitors government policy and procedures on issues affecting international students and academic or administrative visitors from abroad. This is evident in its role in engaging in policy related to immigration law, which regulates international students, researchers and academics.

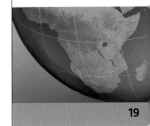

19

REGION:
Sub-Saharan Africa
COUNTRY:
South Africa

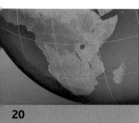

1   As of 2010, Southern African Development Community (SADC) has 15 Member States: Angola, Botswana, Democratic Republic of Congo (DRC), Lesotho, Madagascar, Malawi, Mauritius, Mozambique, Namibia, Seychelles, South Africa, Swaziland, United Republic of Tanzania, Zambia and Zimbabwe. (www.sadc.int)

2   These figures include students from Algeria, Burundi, Gabon, Guinea, Madagascar, Nigeria, Rwanda, Sudan, and other African countries.

3   This includes the Americas, Asia, Europe, and Oceania.

4   Current legislation does not permit private institutions to be called universities; hence official data of student enrollment normally does not include these institutions. It is anticipated that these numbers may be incorporated in the wider data collection effort in the future. At the IEASA annual conference held at the University of the Witwatersrand, Johannesburg on August 31, 2010, the Deputy Director General of the Department of Higher Education indicated that collection of data pertaining to international students from all institutions, private and public, would be in the interest of the government to more fully understand and be better prepared to engage with the unique needs of their students.

REGION: **The Americas**

After Europe, the Americas host the largest number of international students, but have a low outbound mobility ratio compared to other world regions. The United States is the largest host in the region, with 20 percent of the global market share of international students. In academic year 2009/10, the U.S. hosted over 690,000 international students, who represent less than four percent of U.S. higher education enrollments. The largest number of students came from China, India and South Korea. National-level statistics on U.S. students studying abroad, collected by the Institute of International Education (IIE) in its annual *Open Doors Report,* show that over 260,000 U.S. students participated in study abroad programs for academic credit in 2008/09, an increase of close to 150 percent over the previous decade. Approximately ten percent of U.S. undergraduate students study abroad, mostly in non-degree and short-term programs. Recent years have seen a growing participation in programs located in non-traditional destinations outside of Western Europe. The challenge for international education in the United States is twofold: to continue to maintain its competitive advantage in attracting international students and to encourage more U.S. students to study abroad in diverse destinations, including more students from diverse backgrounds and majors.

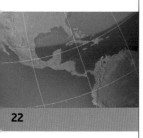

International students in Canada come from over 200 different countries and comprise about eight percent of Canadian undergraduate university students and nearly 20 percent of the graduate student body. In 2009/10 there were over 161,000 international students pursuing higher education in Canada. China, South Korea and the United States are the top three places of origin of international students in Canada, with China sending roughly one-fourth of the overall total. Indian students rank fourth in the total number of international students in Canada, and to increase enrollment efforts, Canadian and Indian universities are taking initiative to increase cooperation. The Canada Indian Educational Council (CIEC) seeks to strengthen the ties between Canadian and Indian universities and promote Canada as a strong study abroad option to Indian students. Canada is also expanding opportunities for its students to participate in study abroad educational and professional experiences.[1]

Canada also has national and institutional policies to attract and retain top academic talent from around the world: according to the Association of Universities and Colleges of Canada (AUCC), as many as 40 percent of Canadian university faculty hold higher education degrees from somewhere other than Canada.

Latin America and the Caribbean experienced a liberalization of higher education in recent years and education systems have converged in the process of increasing internationalization efforts and education quality. National enrollment numbers in the region have increased significantly, leading to the opening of more public and private universities to meet growing demand. The expanding private sector is creating more competition, but the region is still faced with the challenge of expanding higher education, particularly for doctoral programs and post-doctoral research opportunities for students, in order to retain top talent in country and reduce historical "brain drain." To meet these goals, national governments are working on new schemes to offer more institutional and individual funding for higher education.

Although on average only one out of every 100 students studies abroad, this proportion varies a great deal across countries. More students from the Caribbean are mobile than from Central and South America. Nearly 80 percent of students from Latin America who choose to study abroad go to North America or Western Europe for their studies, with Europe becoming increasingly more attractive for Latin American students as universities in the region establish more partnerships with European institutions of higher education. To draw students from the region, the European Commission and national governments are creating more funding opportunities to recruit top talent.

Latin America received two percent of globally mobile students in 2008, with Mexico leading the region as the top host country for international students, with its largest cohort coming from the United States. In 2008/09, more than 40,000 students from the United States studied in Latin America (*Open Doors*, 2010). Universities in Latin America are also forging more regional partnerships and exchange programs, aiming to increase student mobility within Latin America. This trend of intra-regional mobility is reflected in the percentage of students who choose to study outside their home country but within the region, which doubled between 1999 and 2007, from 11 to 23 percent. Chile, Argentina and Venezuela are the top host countries in South America. Brazil is also making strides in internationalization, attracting increasingly more students from the region and beyond. According to UNESCO, Latin America and the Caribbean has the world's largest growth of mobility within their own home region.

As Latin America works to internationalize its higher education institutions, a number of long-standing challenges will have to be addressed. Many countries are in the beginning stages of overcoming the historic educational inequities facing minority and rural populations. Funding for study will continue to be a major concern, as well as providing incentives for students who have studied abroad to return to their home country. As Latin America and the Caribbean reach out to attract international students from other regions, another challenge will be to continue to expand and provide quality education to their own growing university-age population. Inter- and intra-regional exchange is also a significant new trend that requires continued collaborative engagement of various actors in different educational systems.

---

[1] One example is the Students for Development Program (SDP) launched in 2005 that sends higher level students abroad from Canada into developing host destinations for a minimum of three month to undertake internships with partner organizations in one of 26 partner countries around the world. The program is due to expand in 2011 and to bring students from around the world for similar exchanges in Canada.

24

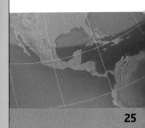

REGION: **The Americas**

COUNTRY: **Canada**

By the Canadian Bureau for International Education (CBIE)

Canada's educational institutions and associations and its governments, federal and provincial, are keenly interested in student mobility. The national organization dedicated exclusively to international education is the Canadian Bureau for International Education (CBIE), an organization that has undertaken major studies concerning Canadian participation in study abroad and international students' experiences in Canada, and is a partner in *Project Atlas*.

While both inbound and outbound mobility are priorities, greater attention has been paid in recent years to attracting international students from other countries. One motivating factor for promoting mobility is the significant contribution to Canadian society. In addition to the benefits that international students receive from a quality education in a multicultural country, their presence strengthens global interconnectedness between Canada and other countries. For educational institutions, international students represent a rich source of new perspectives and research talent. They also often pay higher fees than Canadian students and therefore have a positive impact on an institution's bottom line. Although these financial incentives are present, surveys suggest that institutional leaders believe that academic reasons outweigh economic ones for hosting international students.

The Government of Canada prioritizes inbound mobility for similar reasons. Drawing in new international talent to the academic arena and national labor force is of particular interest due to Canada's demographic reality of increased baby boomer-generation retirements, coupled with a modest

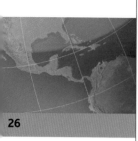

cohort of young labor force entrants. In 2006 a central policy statement known as *Advantage Canada* was issued by Canada's Department of Finance, stating that the Canadian government would increase international student participation in the workforce in several ways, including making it easier for international students to stay in Canada on a long-term basis. Additionally, the off-campus spending of international students presents an important economic motivation.

The Department of Foreign Affairs and International Trade's (DFAIT) International Education and Youth Division is responsible for Canada's foreign policy in the areas of knowledge, learning and the promotion of Canada as a study and research destination. DFAIT elaborated its strong support for inbound mobility with the following rationales:[1]

- Enriched learning and research with international perspectives. As Canada evolves from a resource-based to a knowledge-based economy, the best and brightest from around the world can make a significant contribution to the broad knowledge needed to compete globally, as well as diversifying Canadian campuses, increasing, in turn, the global mindedness of Canadian students, faculty and staff.

- Creation of future partners in trade, political relations and global leadership. Diplomatic and economic ties are strengthened through students who study in Canada and then return home with academic, personal and professional ties that they have made in Canada.

- International students in Canada can work off-campus while studying, helping to fill critical labor market gaps in regions and economic sectors in Canada; and international graduates in Canada are a highly qualified source of potential immigrants to help address skills shortages in Canadian communities.

The legislative environment in Canada favors international student mobility. Citizenship and Immigration Canada (CIC) has over the past few years instituted programs that encourage international students to choose Canada as a study destination, including the Off-Campus Work Permit (OCWP) and making more widely accessible and extending the length of the Post-Graduation Work Permit program (PGWP). CIC has also eased the process for visa applications from international students and reduced processing time for applications and renewals through an online application system.

- There were over 161,000 international students pursuing post-secondary education in Canada in 2009/10.

- In 2009, the top five places of origin were China, South Korea, United States, India and France.

- Over 44,000 students from Canada studied abroad in 2008.

Source: CBIE, UNESCO

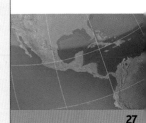

27

REGION:
The Americas
COUNTRY:
Canada

In addition, the application for permanent residency through the Canadian Experience Class program may facilitate international students' migration to Canada as it, along with the other changes in immigration policies, may encourage internationally mobile students to choose Canada as a study destination. The PGWP and OCWP have already proven overwhelmingly popular. In 2008, 16,000 students were granted OCWP, representing about 40 percent of those eligible. In 2008, 18,000 graduates applied for PGWP, up 63 percent from 2007.

A 2009 report commissioned by DFAIT, *The Economic Impact of International Education in Canada*[2] found that $6.5 billion annually is contributed to the Canadian economy from international students through tuition, living costs, travel while in Canada, and visits from family. International students in Canada also annually create 83,000 domestic jobs and contribute $291 million in government revenue.

As part of the promotion of Canada as an education destination, DFAIT has targeted nine priority countries from which to increase student mobility: Brazil, China, France, Germany, India, Japan, South Korea, Mexico, and the U.S.; and four priority regions: members of the Association of Southeast Asian Nations (ASEAN), the Caribbean, the Arabian Gulf and North Africa.

DFAIT's *Education au/in Canada's IMAGINE* is Canada's new international education promotion brand that advertises Canada to prospective international students. The *IMAGINE* brand was launched in 2008 and became available in January 2010 for use by non-governmental actors. Due to its

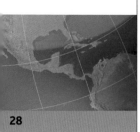

short history, it is not possible to assess the impact the brand has had. However, a 2009 survey by CBIE[3] found that 31 percent of South Korean students studying in Canada who saw advertising about Canada as a study destination reported that the advertising influenced them very much. Similar findings were reported for German, Indian, Japanese, U.S., French and Mexican students.

On the other side of the mobility picture, study abroad by Canadian students offers the opportunity for major enhancements to their educational, personal and professional development. Specifically, both higher education institutions and the governments of Canada promote study abroad for domestic students to encourage increased language capability and cultural sensitivity; an expanded view of the world; and building a future network of internationalized intellectuals. All of this helps to ensure that Canadians are global citizens and can cooperate as well as compete internationally.

Together with governments and associations, CBIE works in a variety of ways to support and promote student mobility in Canada and encourages Canadian and international students to study, work and conduct research

facts and figures

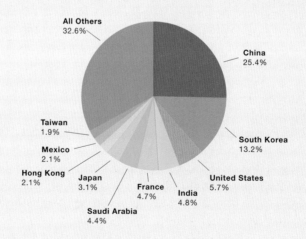

Figure 2: Places of Origin of International Students in Canada, 2009

Source: CBIE

abroad. To this end, CBIE administers a range of programs and initiatives for both cohorts.

Although CBIE and Canada are committed to a *global* approach, recently Canada's government launched a major strategy for the Americas. On behalf of DFAIT, CBIE administers scholarships to promote mobility within the Americas: the Emerging Leaders in the Americas Program; the Canada-Chile Leadership Program and the Canada-CARICOM Leadership Program, among others. These programs advance the Canadian government's strategy by supporting human capital development and a new generation of leaders in the Americas, while strengthening linkages between Canadian institutions and those in partner countries in the hemisphere. Numerous other programs are offered for students from Commonwealth countries, and from Asia, Africa and Europe.

CBIE hosts an Annual Conference focused on mobility. In addition to timely policy and practice sessions, the Conference has included a forum specific to a particular country or region for the past three years. In 2007, the forum focused on India, followed by Latin America and the Caribbean, and China. In October 2010, CBIE collaborated with the Inter-American Organization for Higher Education Collaboration (IOHE) and the Consortium for North American Higher Education (CONAHEC) in hosting the inaugural Conference of the Americas on International Education[4] in Calgary, Alberta. The Conference, "Internationalization: Essential Building Block to Quality in 21st Century Education," provided a space for connecting with partners and for incubating new opportunities and ideas across the hemisphere.

CBIE also provides research and statistics on topical issues to support recommendations for increased student mobility. CBIE's 2009 study of the international student experience revealed improvements in a number of areas with respect to international students in Canada, highlighted some challenges, and provided an evidence base for policy recommendations. CBIE's publication, *World of Learning: Canadian Postsecondary Students and the Study Abroad Experience*, provides a status assessment of Canadian students' participation in study abroad, polls the Canadian public, employers, faculty, staff and students across Canada on their attitudes towards study abroad, and makes recommendations to improve the rate of participation in study abroad programs. CBIE's research is disseminated widely throughout the education community.

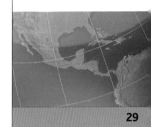

29

REGION:
The Americas
COUNTRY:
Canada

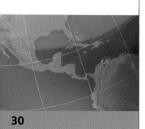

Overall, Canada's support for international education mobility is following a positive trend. In 2010, CBIE and four other national education associations established the Canadian Consortium for International Education Marketing (CCIEM) as a signal of their commitment to working together to attract the best and the brightest students from around the world to Canada. In addition, the past few years—since 2005—have seen enhanced interest on the part of governments, both federal and provincial, who have undertaken more in-depth research, provided greater investment in promotion and scholarships, and improved employment opportunities for international students. Increasingly, federal and provincial governments are working collaboratively and are engaging the national and provincial organizations in this enterprise.

Over the coming years, international education organizations and institutions can expect heightened Canadian presence in world education events, more robust scholarship offerings, and smoother processing of study permits and work permits for international students. At the same time, associations will be paying more attention to the professional development of international educators, as they look toward institutions and the government to respond with equal support and commitment, while also recognizing the importance of the international education field to mobility and partnership building.

Canadian Bureau for International Education: The Canadian Bureau for International Education (CBIE) is a national, bilingual, not-for-profit, membership organization dedicated to promotion of Canada's international relations through international education.

---

[1] Tools and Services You Can Use (Greenshields, C., 2009), http://www.languagescanada.ca/files/DFAIT%20Presentation%20Calgary%202009.pdf

[2] The Economic Impact of International Education in Canada (Department of Foreign Affairs and International Trade Canada, 2009); http://www.international.gc.ca/education/reports-rapports.aspx?lang=eng

[3] Canada First: The 2009 Survey of International Students in Canada (CBIE, 2009).

[4] Conference of the Americas on International Education, www.caie-caei.org.

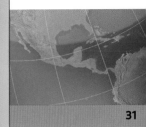

REGION: **The Americas**

COUNTRY: **Mexico**

By National Association of Universities and Higher Education Institutions (ANUIES)

31

REGION:
The Americas
COUNTRY:
Mexico

Mexico's government promotes inbound student mobility in order to diversify Mexico's student population and enhance the academic campus and culture. Both inbound and outbound forms of mobility allow for students to develop cultural perspectives and broaden their understanding of languages, and cultural, economic, and business patterns of other countries. International students benefit from a flexible culture within Mexican universities, particularly in regards to the recognition of previous courses of study and degrees obtained in other countries. Mexican students who study abroad are generally graduate-level students. The high-quality training these students receive abroad in priority disciplines contributes to capacity building and human resource development in Mexico.

On a regional level, Mexico's Department of Foreign Affairs implements a scholarship program for undergraduate and graduate students from Central and South America and the Caribbean. This program not only strengthens the cultural ties Mexico has forged with Latin American and Caribbean countries, but consolidates the solidarity expressed to countries that have a lower socio-economic development than Mexico.

Through the National Council for Science and Technology (CONACYT), the government has supported initiatives to advance an internationalization policy for Mexico. Two such initiatives that CONACYT manages focus on student mobility; the third, Mexico's National System of Researchers (SNI), supports researchers locally in the form of monthly stipends and tiered official recognition through a robust evaluation process.

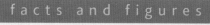
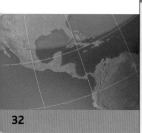

32

REGION:
The Americas
COUNTRY:
Mexico

- There were more than 2,000 international students in Mexico in 2007.[1]

- The top five places of origin in 2007 were the United States, France, Canada, Spain and Germany.

- The National Council for Science and Technology (CONACYT) implements mobility scholarship programs and grants formal recognition to international programs for institutions.

- The National Association of Universities and Higher Education Institutions (ANUIES) is the primary organization responsible for higher education data collection in Mexico, representing the full range of public and private institutions.

Source: ANUIES

CONACYT also funds an international scholarship program to support outbound student mobility, mainly at the Ph.D. level but also at the Master's degree level. Priority is given to areas of study in science and technology, including biotechnology, medicine, energy, environment, manufacturing technologies, materials, nanotechnology, information technology and telecommunications, and applied mathematics and modeling.

The second policy that supports mobility, the National Register of Quality Post-graduate Programs, is geared toward inbound student mobility. On a yearly basis, universities can apply to have their programs evaluated. The programs therefore are designated under the following categories: "recent creation"; "in the process of becoming consolidated"; "consolidated"; or "internationally proficient." In this way, CONACYT has created a national standard through which universities can certify their programs and come closer to increasing their international desirability.

Immigration and Mobility within the Americas
Mexico's immigration policy does not hinder student mobility, with the National Immigration Institute (INM) implementing recent reforms to facilitate the legal processes for incoming students. The latest modification waives visa fees for international students. Nevertheless, significant

challenges still exist for students from some Latin American countries that typically send students to Mexico, such as Colombia and Bolivia.

The National Association of Universities and Higher Education Institutions (ANUIES) has focused on promoting short-term student and faculty mobility through the implementation of exchange programs. ANUIES has been involved with government agencies such as the Ministry of Education (SEP) and CONACYT in the creation of programs that promote academic mobility, especially among researcher and lecturer networks. ANUIES supports its affiliates by creating and strengthening international cooperation networks through a variety of programs and activities.

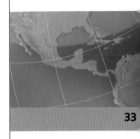

Specifically, ANUIES:
- Develops cooperation programs with international counterparts, expanding opportunities for student and academic mobility and joint research programs.
- Promotes the international cooperation of affiliates through events, presidents meetings, and courses.
- Strengthens inter-institutional relationships (university associations, president missions, etc.).
- Offers academic cooperation courses for affiliates.
- Manages distribution lists with information about grants, academic opportunities, and scholarships.

ANUIES has partnered with neighboring countries to promote student mobility within Latin America. One particular academic cooperation agreement that has been very successful and which continues to grow is with Argentina's Inter-University Council (CIN). Signed in 2006, the bilateral program, JIMA, originally included eight universities, four from each country. It now involves 30 institutions and at least 60 students per semester, and has expanded to include a faculty and staff mobility program (MAGMA).

Another successful regional program managed by ANUIES is a student exchange program with Quebec and its Conference of University Presidents and Principals (CREPUQ). Signed in 1994, it is geared mainly toward undergraduate students, though graduate students do complete exchange programs as well. Although CREPUQ manages a multilateral program, at

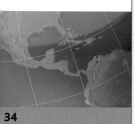

34

REGION:
The Americas
COUNTRY:
Mexico

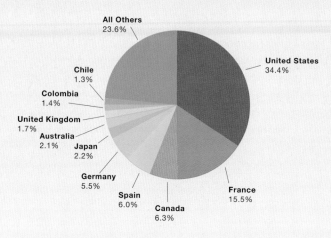

All Others
23.6%

United States
34.4%

Chile
1.3%

Colombia
1.4%

United Kingdom
1.7%

Australia
2.1%

Japan
2.2%

Germany
5.5%

Spain
6.0%

Canada
6.3%

France
15.5%

Figure 3: Places of Origin of International Students in Mexico, 2007
Source: ANUIES

the bilateral level between Mexico and Canada, 58 Mexican and 20 Canadian institutions are involved. Data collected from 2000 to 2009 shows that a total of 652 Mexican students completed an exchange in Canada, and 392 Canadian students completed an exchange in Mexico.

Additionally, ANUIES has partnered with other Latin American institutions through networks created by the European Union's ALFA III program. Currently, ANUIES is involved in a project with 32 institutions from 17 countries including: Argentina, Bolivia, Brazil, Chile, Colombia, Costa Rica, Ecuador, Nicaragua, Paraguay, Peru, Uruguay and Venezuela; and from Europe: Austria, Italy, Portugal and Spain. The project concludes in 2011 and aims to produce an analysis of current bi- and multi-regional academic and social cooperation structures, and a proposed design for a horizontal cooperation structure that will allow academic initiatives to filter through multiple levels of a particular country (for example, across federal and local governments, non-profit organizations, higher education institutions, community groups, etc.).

An important benefit of these collaborations has been the creation of a forum that allows for and encourages the exchange of information among the countries involved—not only to better understand each other's educational systems, but also to find ways to consolidate initiatives that can further promote academic cooperation at a regional level. The challenge has been to overcome fragmented governmental structures that still have not fully developed and the forestalling of appropriate funding to support policies that emphasize the importance of academic internationalization.

Several surveys have been developed to study various academic and student mobility programs, particularly those involving short-term exchanges. ANUIES has also initiated an effort to collect and maintain data on student mobility, which has to date been non-existent in Mexico. ANUIES hopes to systematize this process and solidify the best practices among affiliated higher education institutions by constantly monitoring the spectrum of international cooperation.

The *National Association of Universities and Higher Education Institutions (ANUIES):* ANUIES is the primary organization responsible for data collection in Mexico.

---

[1]   This data does not include all international students pursuing degree and non-degree programs.

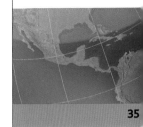

REGION:
The Americas
COUNTRY:
Mexico

36

REGION: **The Americas**

COUNTRY: **United States**

By the Institute of International Education (IIE)

REGION:
The Americas
COUNTRY:
United States

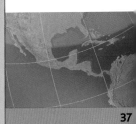

Since the 1950's, the United States has been the leading destination for international students, and it continues to host an increasing number of students and scholars from around the world. In 2009/10, according to IIE's *Open Doors Report*, there were over 690,000 international students studying in the U.S. and an additional 115,000 international scholars doing research or teaching on campuses across the country. For decades, numerous initiatives sponsored by the U.S. government, foundations, non-governmental organizations (NGOs), as well as both public and private universities and colleges, have contributed to the internationalization of higher education in the United States. The reputation of the United States as a global leader in higher education and training, combined with its vast number of accredited higher education institutions and flexible degree programs catering to all types of students, has created opportunities for a growing number of international and U.S. students to gain international experience.

With over 4,000 public and private higher education institutions in the United States, no single federal agency is solely responsible for internationalizing the higher education sphere and efforts are most often led by individual educational institutions. Internationalization strategies at U.S. universities and colleges are decided institutionally (or even at the departmental or faculty level), and efforts to attract international students are initiated through global outreach programs, recruiting events, alumni networking, and scholarship and funding incentives provided by the host campus. Additionally, the active U.S. NGO sector provides numerous services that help campuses internationalize, informs prospective international students

38

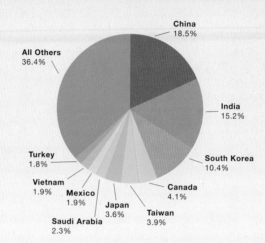

Figure 4: Places of Origin of International Students in the United States, 2009/10

Source: *Open Doors, 2010*

about higher education in the United States, and offers programs ranging from short-term educational and cultural exchanges to support for degree-seeking international students.

U.S. students are also increasingly participating in international academic programs. In the last twenty years, the number of U.S. students studying abroad has more than tripled, with 260,327 U.S. students studying abroad for academic credit in 2008/09, according to *Open Doors*. While the majority continue to study in Europe, more U.S. students are studying in non-traditional destinations in Africa, Asia, Latin America and the Middle East. The U.S. universities and colleges that sponsor study abroad programs are increasingly diversifying their programs to include new destinations and short-term study opportunities (eight weeks or less) to engage more of their students in international educational exchange.

National Efforts to Internationalize Higher Education
International Students Studying in the U.S.

For decades, the U.S. government has worked to ensure that international students continue to feel welcome, while also promoting study abroad programs for U.S. students. A number of federal agencies have mandates to support international education and exchange programs, including offices within the U.S. Department of State, Department of Education, Department of Defense, and the U.S. Agency for International Development (USAID), among others.

The U.S. Department of State plays a key role in promoting U.S. higher education internationally and study abroad programs for students from the United States. With support from the U.S. Department of State's Bureau of Educational and Cultural Affairs (ECA), over 400 EducationUSA advising centers worldwide serve prospective students seeking higher education opportunities in the United States, and promote U.S. study abroad in their home country. EducationUSA is a global network of advisers who provide free, comprehensive, and impartial information on accredited higher education institutions in the U.S. Today, there are EducationUSA offices in 169 countries, with experts who are able to help students identify the U.S. institutions that best fit their academic goals, and mesh their preparation within the local educational system with the requirements for admission to U.S. colleges and universities. The advisers' familiarity with the local higher education community also serves as a resource to U.S. institutions exploring opportunities to expand their internationalization efforts and study abroad programs for U.S. students. U.S. higher education institutions and

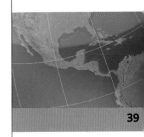

39

REGION:
The Americas
COUNTRY:
United States

facts and figures

- Over 690,000 international students studied in the U.S. in 2009/10.

- China, India, South Korea, Canada and Taiwan were the top places of origin in 2009/10, accounting for over 52 percent of the international students studying in the U.S.

- Over 260,000 U.S. students studied abroad for academic credit in 2008/09.

- The Institute of International Education has reported annual international student mobility data for the U.S. through its *Open Doors Report* for over 60 years.

Source: *Open Doors* Report 2010, IIE

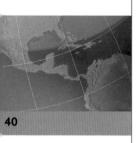

40

REGION:
The Americas
COUNTRY:
United States

NGOs partner with EducationUSA in organizing international college fairs and informational sessions for students from around the world. A network of Regional Educational Advising Coordinators (REACs) provides training and maintains standards for EducationUSA centers.

In addition to supporting efforts to increase knowledge abroad about higher education in the U.S., the U.S. Government also invests in publicly-funded scholarships, fellowships, and international educational and cultural exchange programs. The largest and most prominent of these is the U.S. Department of State's Fulbright Program, funded annually by Congress, with cost-sharing from many other countries and host universities, and administered by the Institute of International Education (IIE), an independent not-for-profit organization headquartered in New York City. This flagship program is the largest federally-funded educational exchange program in the U.S., providing funding for students, educators, and professionals annually to engage in international educational exchange at the graduate and post-doctoral level. The program supports over 7,000 U.S. and international students and scholars annually for study, teaching, or research outside their home countries. Established after World War II as a vehicle for building mutual understanding, the Fulbright Program also includes leadership initiatives and community engagement activities that augment the academic programs geared toward students and young professionals in a wide range of academic and professional fields. The program has grown in recent years to include over 150 countries; a special program for outstanding international Ph.D. candidates in science and technology fields; Fulbright English Teaching Assistantship (ETA) opportunities in 65 countries; and Fulbright Foreign Language Teaching Assistantship (FLTA) grants, which support the teaching of critical languages at colleges and universities throughout the United States. Federal funding for Fulbright and other exchange programs has expanded, as has cost-sharing by partner countries.

Over the past decade, U.S. national policies have encouraged the expansion of student and scholar mobility and exchange. At a policy level, changes to visa regulations have allowed international students to stay in the country for an extended period of time for Optional Practical Training (OPT), including up to 29 months for graduates in science, technology, engineering, or mathematics (STEM) fields. Consular offices have also streamlined the student visa application process—particularly in key sending countries such as China and India—by employing additional staff, expanding office hours and posting regular updates on waiting times for interviews and appointments on their websites.

U.S. Study Abroad

Study abroad is also a focus of U.S. internationalization efforts. National and institutional goals for expanding and diversifying study abroad opportunities are driven by the need to create more globally informed U.S. citizens, increase expertise in critical foreign languages, and prepare graduates for professional engagement and participation in an interconnected world.

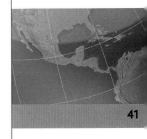

Today, minority students represent less than 20 percent of U.S. students who study abroad, while comprising 36 percent of students in higher education overall. Students in the social sciences still comprise the largest proportion of students who participate in study abroad programs, while students in STEM fields are underrepresented in study abroad programs. A number of national scholarship and fellowship programs supported by the U.S. government help achieve these goals and promote greater participation, particularly among groups traditionally underrepresented in study abroad. The Benjamin A. Gilman Scholarship Program, sponsored by the ECA, provides grants of up to one academic year of study to support U.S. students with financial need who otherwise could not study abroad at the undergraduate level. More than 2,300 of these scholarships will be awarded in 2010/11, with over 60 percent awarded to minority students. Over half of Gilman awardees study outside of Western Europe, which traditionally hosts the majority of U.S. students abroad. The program offers enhancement awards for the study of critical languages and encourages students in STEM fields.

Having citizens who are more proficient in the world's languages is critical to U.S. national interests, and several programs have been established by various agencies to support intensive language study. One of the largest is the David L. Boren Scholarship and Fellowship program, which receives funding from the National Security Education Program and provides nearly 300 grants each year to undergraduate and graduate students to study strategically important languages throughout Africa, Asia, Central and Eastern Europe, Latin America and the Middle East. The U.S. Department of State and the U.S. Department of Education also fund study abroad to promote enhanced foreign language competence, especially in critical language areas. A successful example is the

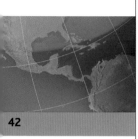

Critical Language Scholarship (CLS) Programs, sponsored by the U.S. Department of State, which offers intensive summer institutes in 13 critical languages for U.S. undergraduate and graduate students.

State and Campus Efforts in Internationalization

More than a dozen states have active state or regional consortia designed to collectively promote their states as destinations for international students. With brands like *Destination Indiana*, *Discover Ohio*, and the Philadelphia area's *One Big Campus*, states and cities are taking steps to internationalize their campuses and raise their global profile.

At the institutional level, campuses across the U.S. are increasing their internationalization efforts, taking proactive measures to promote study abroad, attract international students and foster collaborative relationships with foreign institutions, which result in an exchange of knowledge and human capital. Some campuses have established fully staffed "gateway offices" abroad to provide information on application procedure and study in the United States. Institutions of higher education are also improving the international student experience with the strengthening of international student offices or centers, unique international student orientation and community engagement programs, and support for international students for the duration of their studies in the United States. Some state universities waive the higher out-of-state tuition rate as an incentive to attract more international students. Universities and colleges are also expanding study abroad program offerings, granting academic credit for a wide range of programs, from short faculty-led visits to semester- or year-long enrollment in the programs of partner universities abroad. Short-term and summer study abroad programs are increasingly available in a wide range of fields for students who are unable to go for a semester or year-long program for financial, academic, or personal reasons.

Institutions are also making strategic efforts to establish long-term institutional partnerships and expand collaborative research projects. A number of U.S. universities have set up branch campuses and joint- or dual-degree programs around the world to attract more international students and provide opportunities for U.S. students to study abroad. Others are expanding use of distance learning and technology to connect students at home and around the world.

The Role of the NGO Sector

The non-profit non-governmental sector in the United States plays a significant role in internationalizing higher education. The collaboration between U.S. government entities and NGOs as well as between NGOs and higher education institutions provides additional programmatic and informational resources in support of study abroad, international education, and institutional partnerships around the world.

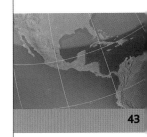

A vital network of NGOs and membership associations represent a wide range of higher education institutions along with stakeholders in the public and private sector. Many of these organizations collaborate to promote and advocate for internationalization on the national level, often through the Alliance for International Educational and Cultural Exchange, an association of over 70 NGOs comprising the international educational and cultural exchange community in the United States. In addition to the Institute of International Education, these organizations include, among others, the American Association of Community Colleges (AACC), the American Association of State Colleges and Universities (AASCU), the American Council on Education (ACE), the Association of American Universities (AAU), the Association of Public and Land-grant Universities (APLU), the College Board, the Council of Graduate Schools (CGS) and NAFSA: Association of International Educators. In different ways and at various levels, these organizations and others promote academic mobility and involve their member institutions in advocacy, research, and programs to support international education at the post-secondary level. Both independently and collaboratively, these organizations contribute to training and raising standards of excellence in internationalization activities on campuses and to spearheading national campaigns that increase support for international education and exchange programs worldwide.

The Institute of International Education (IIE) is the largest nonprofit organization in the U.S. devoted to international educational exchanges. IIE collaborates with governments, foundations and other sponsors to create and manage programs of study and training for students, educators and professionals from all sectors. These programs include the flagship Fulbright Program and Gilman Scholarships, administered on behalf of the U.S. Department of State, and the National Security Education Program's Boren Scholarships and Fellowships. IIE also conducts policy

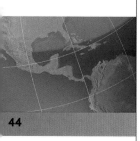

REGION:
The Americas
COUNTRY:
United States

research, provides resources on international exchange opportunities to a membership base of over 1,100 institutions of higher education and other organizations, and offers a safe haven for scholars in danger around the globe through IIE's Scholar Rescue Fund.

IIE's new Center for International Partnerships in Higher Education, launched with grant support from the U.S. Department of Education's Fund for the Improvement of Postsecondary Education (FIPSE), assists U.S. colleges and universities with developing and sustaining institutional partnerships around the world. In November 2010, IIE led a delegation of 30 U.S. college and university presidents and senior international officers to India for meetings with Indian counterparts about future bilateral academic collaborations. A similar trip to China will be held in May 2011, building on the experience of IIE delegates to Indonesia, Russia, Mexico and other countries. IIE also offers training in scholarship management, faculty, and other internationalization strategies to non-U.S. universities and governments through its Center for Higher Education Capacity Development.

IIE has also been a pioneer in researching academic mobility in higher education. For over 60 years, IIE's annual research publication on mobility statistics in the United States, *Open Doors Report on International Educational Exchange*, supported by the Bureau of Educational and Cultural Affairs of the U.S. Department of State, has served as a key resource to policymakers and stakeholders in the higher education field.

The goal of *Project Atlas*, which IIE launched in 2001 with funding from the Ford Foundation, is to collect and disseminate accurate, timely and consistent data on global student mobility. The Project's associated website—the *Atlas of Student Mobility*—highlights country-level data shared by 21 partner countries and national academic mobility agencies around the world. Supported by the U.S. Department of State and participating organizations in partner countries, the Project also provides important resources for researchers and policymakers to understand student mobility trends and examine the broader implications of global student migration.

REGION: **Asia**

Students from Asia comprise the largest group of globally mobile students around the world (43 percent). Students from China (820,000) represent 25 percent of the global total of international students and over 268,000 Indian students are enrolled in higher education institutions (HEIs) around the world. After sub-Saharan Africa, Central Asia has one of the highest outbound mobility ratios in the world: five out of every 100 students from this sub-region study overseas. In contrast, only two out of every 100 students from East Asia and the Pacific study outside their home countries; the ratio is even lower for South and West Asia at 1.5 percent (UNESCO, 2010).

While many countries in the region have experienced "brain drain" in the past, a number of Asian countries have recently emerged as important higher education destinations, attracting large numbers of students not just within the region but also from Europe and North America. The most notable example is China, which in 2008/09 hosted over 238,000 international students. Most international students in China pursue their studies in non-degree programs, and come from neighboring Asian countries, the U.S. and Russia. However, as China, India, and other Asian countries implement

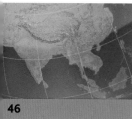

national policies that create more educational opportunities and as more of their higher education institutions achieve world-class status, it is expected that more international students will be attracted to enroll in degree programs.

Countries in Southeast Asia, including Malaysia, Singapore, and Thailand are also actively promoting their universities as host destinations as well as encouraging large numbers of their own students to study abroad. Some countries in Southeast Asia that have traditionally had lower outbound mobility have seen increases in recent years. Nepal and Vietnam are two notable examples of significant growth in studying abroad for higher education, both outside of the region and within it. Japan has experienced the reverse trend, a steep decline in its students studying abroad outside of the region, although significant numbers continue to study in China. In recent years, the Japanese government launched an initiative to increase the incoming international student population to 300,000 over ten years, hoping to nearly triple the current number of international students (132,000 as of May 2009). The efforts to accomplish this goal include encouraging universities to partner with higher education institutions overseas and providing both merit and Japanese government-based scholarships to attract international students.

As the demand for higher education in Asia rises, new types of educational opportunities are being created. After the Middle East, Asia is the largest host region for branch campuses of foreign universities, with Singapore and Malaysia as two prominent examples in Southeast Asia. The growing economies of Southeast Asian countries have also facilitated an expansion of non-degree higher education programs, including skills training and executive education to meet the demands of transitioning from labor to knowledge economies. As new types of education programs become more commonplace, the traditional public higher educational institution is challenged to keep up with the growing needs of the market economy and to compete with the private higher education sector.

In recent years, a number of Asian countries have initiated reforms to liberalize the system of higher education. This has resulted in an expansion of the private sector for higher education as well as more partnerships between local and international educational institutions. As Asian countries focus on developing world-class universities and attracting more international students, education quality remains a core challenge and the focal point of educational development in the region. Regional mobility associations are a key component in these efforts. The Asia-Pacific Association for International Education (APAIE), an international non-profit comprised of university representatives dedicated to promoting the internationalization of higher education in the Asia Pacific region, collaborates with University Mobility in Asia and the Pacific (UMAP), which is comprised of government and non-government representatives of the higher education sector in the Asia/Pacific region. The Southeast Asian Ministers of Education Organization (SEAMEO) is a 45-year old organization that aims to "promote cooperation in education, science and culture in the Southeast Asian region," emphasizing the importance of intraregional cooperation. Together, these associations are creating momentum for partnerships between Asia and the world and are aiding in the process of internationalization of higher education.

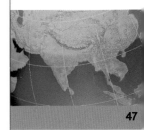

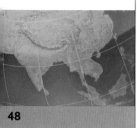

48

REGION: Asia

COUNTRY: China

By China Scholarship Council (CSC)

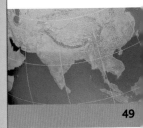

China is a major source of the world's global student population, and is fast becoming a hub for regional and global mobility to its higher education institutions.

Through its scholarship and educational policy arm, the China Scholarship Council (CSC), the Chinese government supports inbound and outbound mobility to:

- Promote Chinese culture.
- Foster people-to-people communication between foreign countries and China.
- Enhance the competitiveness and internationalization of Chinese higher education.
- Stimulate Sino-foreign educational exchanges and scientific research collaborations.
- Cultivate creative and international talent through overseas education of Chinese students and scholars.

Over the past two decades, the Chinese government has enacted a series of national policies to increasingly promote student mobility. In 1992, it first established a policy of supporting overseas study, encouraging graduates to return home and allowing scholars to spend time abroad and return to the country freely. The CSC is one of the key entities responsible for implementing this policy on the government's behalf.

50

REGION:
Asia
COUNTRY:
China

Since its founding in 1996, CSC has adhered to the principles of "individual application, expert evaluation, fair competition, [and] selection by merit and bonded sponsorship." CSC is composed of a secretariat and a committee consisting of fifteen members, including the Ministry of Education, Ministry of Finance, Ministry of Foreign Affairs, Ministry of Human Resources and Social Security, Ministry of Public Security, Chinese Academy of Sciences, Chinese Academy of Engineering, Chinese Academy of Social Sciences, National Development and Reform Commission, and National Foundation for Natural Sciences.

As entrusted by the Ministry of Education, the Secretariat is responsible for implementing programs in both study abroad affairs and study in China affairs. Through its eight divisions and offices, CSC is responsible for collecting and compiling data relevant to Chinese government scholarship programs for both inbound and outbound student mobility, which is reported to the Ministry of Education for policy making.

Outbound Mobility: Scholarships and Programs
CSC works in a number of ways to support outbound Chinese student mobility, a central activity involving the administration of national scholarship programs. CSC provides 12,000 scholarships annually to Chinese citizens for study overseas. In addition, CSC has established a special program that provides state scholarships to high-achieving self-financed students studying abroad through a competitive selection process. Since its implementation in 2003, over 1,400 Chinese students have been awarded these scholarships. The program reflects the government's concern towards and support of self-financed students and has proven to be an immensely popular opportunity among Chinese students studying overseas. As of November 2009, 58,419 Chinese citizens have been granted government scholarships to study abroad with an average return rate of 97 percent. Most scholars who return after an overseas study experience have played a key role in various fields toward national capacity building in China.

For China, regional student mobility among neighboring countries represents another key facet of international exchange, which helps facilitate the mutual recognition of degrees, certificates and academic credits. In response to a significant imbalance in both the economic and the science-technology sectors between neighboring countries, the Chinese government is making strides to send more Chinese students to regional institutions for their study abroad experiences, with the goal of improved regional economic development, social cohesion and stability. CSC leverages the Chinese government's educational and cultural agreements with foreign governments and sponsored scholarships to encourage study in neighboring countries, particularly among students and scholars whose research focuses on regional or linguistic issues.

In cooperation with its foreign partners beyond the Asia region, CSC has held a Sino-Foreign University President's Meeting, as well as the International Graduate Scholarship Conferences as mechanisms to support Chinese student educational opportunities abroad. Every October, CSC organizes an annual International Graduate Scholarship Fair represented by world-renowned foreign universities and top students from leading Chinese universities who pursue doctoral studies overseas.

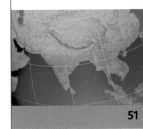

51

REGION:
Asia
COUNTRY:
China

facts and figures

- There were over 238,000 international students in China in 2008/09.

- The top five places of origin in 2008/09 were South Korea, United States, Japan, Vietnam and Thailand.

- A total of 820,000 Chinese students studied abroad, including approximately 229,000 students who began their studies abroad in 2009.

- The China Scholarship Council administers scholarships and data collection on behalf of the Chinese Ministry of Education.

Source: CSC

Inbound Mobility

China now represents one of the top destinations in Asia for inbound international students. The Chinese government's support of inbound mobility aims to promote China and its programs as a leading study abroad destination. As with outbound mobility funding programs, the CSC is responsible for overseeing government and other sponsored scholarships for international students to study at Chinese universities. Approximately 20,000 scholarships

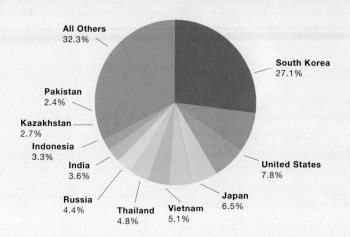

All Others
32.3%

South Korea
27.1%

Pakistan
2.4%

Kazakhstan
2.7%

Indonesia
3.3%

India
3.6%

United States
7.8%

Russia
4.4%

Thailand
4.8%

Vietnam
5.1%

Japan
6.5%

Figure 5: Places of Origin of International Students in China, 2008/09
Source: CSC

are granted annually to international students to further their education in China.

Since 2008, all 985 Project[1] universities have been entrusted to independently recruit and grant government scholarships to foreign students interested in graduate studies in China. At the same time, nine provinces and autonomous regions have been authorized to independently recruit and grant government scholarships to foreign students from neighboring countries interested in pursuing graduate studies in China. Further, since 2002, CSC has organized China's Higher Education Exhibitions in more than 20 countries and regions in the world, attracting large numbers of potential students interested in studying in China.

Partnerships with institutions and organizations overseas have created additional opportunities in faculty training and professional development. For example, the Study Abroad Program for Young Backbone Teachers in Chinese Universities has annually sponsored 1,500 teachers from 211 Project universities allowing them to make scholarly visits to foreign universities. In addition, since 2007, CSC, in cooperation with

985 Project universities, has selected 5,000 students per year to pursue doctoral degrees or carry out dissertation research at foreign institutions. The CSC has signed 77 cooperative agreements with internationally renowned higher education institutions.

Despite the global financial crisis in 2008-09, China has made a remarkable contribution to promoting international student mobility. In 2009, its yearly number of outbound students reached a record-high of 229,000, while the number of inbound international students in China exceeded 230,000 for the first time. This two-way exchange has been greatly beneficial to the promotion of Chinese traditional culture, mutual understanding and solidarity between Chinese and foreign people; the formation of the world's impression of Chinese national characteristics of diligence, wisdom, smartness, persistence and tolerance and also the recognition of the quality and standard of the Chinese higher education system among the international community.

According to the Ministry's forthcoming "State Guidelines for Middle- and Long-Term Educational Reform and Development Plan (Year 2010-2020)," over the next few years, China will continue with its policy of educating a considerable number of students, scholars and professionals overseas, who can engage fully and actively in global affairs and academia. In the meantime, China aims to further enlarge the scale of international students studying in China and increase the number of Chinese government scholarships offered to them, so as to improve the level of China's engagement in global educational cooperation and exchanges.

China Scholarship Council (CSC): China Scholarship Council (CSC) is a not-for-profit organization with legal person status affiliated with the Ministry of Education in China. CSC promotes international student mobility by supporting Chinese students to study overseas and foreign students to study in China.

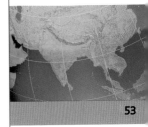

REGION:
Asia
COUNTRY:
China

----

[1]   Project of the Government to promote the Chinese higher education system.

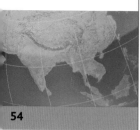

54

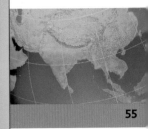

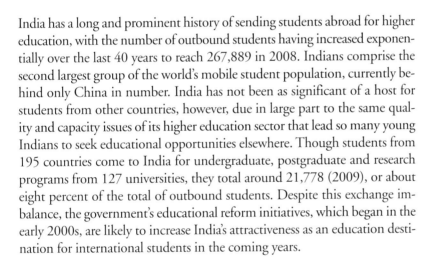

REGION: **Asia**

COUNTRY: **India**[1]

India has a long and prominent history of sending students abroad for higher education, with the number of outbound students having increased exponentially over the last 40 years to reach 267,889 in 2008. Indians comprise the second largest group of the world's mobile student population, currently behind only China in number. India has not been as significant of a host for students from other countries, however, due in large part to the same quality and capacity issues of its higher education sector that lead so many young Indians to seek educational opportunities elsewhere. Though students from 195 countries come to India for undergraduate, postgraduate and research programs from 127 universities, they total around 21,778 (2009), or about eight percent of the total of outbound students. Despite this exchange imbalance, the government's educational reform initiatives, which began in the early 2000s, are likely to increase India's attractiveness as an education destination for international students in the coming years.

The economic boom in India over the last two decades, in conjunction with the priority the fast growing Indian middle class places on quality educational opportunities for their children, has created a national imperative to improve the capacity of the education sector. The Indian higher education sector is one of the largest in the world with 532 universities and 25,951 colleges; yet the demand for higher education still far exceeds the available supply. There are over 600 million Indians under the age of 25, but less than 12 percent have access to higher education in the country. Further, due to structural deficiencies in the areas of teaching quality, research performance, governance, and graduate outcomes and

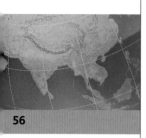

employability, the opportunities for quality higher education are reduced even further. As a result, large numbers of India's elite and middle-class students head abroad for higher education, with the United States, Australia and the United Kingdom as top destinations.

In response to these demographic and infrastructural challenges, the government proposed and implemented a number of key initiatives in the last decade to transform the higher education sector. These initiatives are intended not only to address the quality and capacity issues needed to provide a competitive education for a greater number of domestic students, but also in direct and indirect ways to make India a more desirable destination for students from other countries and to create further linkages between institutions.

Bolstered by the high priority India's Prime Minister, Dr. Manmohan Singh, has placed on improving the educational system, the government has made a number of efforts to internationalize the higher education sector. The long-standing University Grants Commission (UGC) indicated in its planning document of 2000 that a policy was needed to promote inbound and outbound student flows. UGC implemented a coordination system for promoting Indian higher education in 2004/05, though it has seen limited success in increasing recruitments. For example, the Indian Council for Cultural Relations, the government's public diplomacy division, recruits about one thousand students each year.

In 2005, the government formed the National Knowledge Commission (NKC) to advise the Prime Minister on educational policy toward furthering the improvement of the educational sector, resulting in a number of policy recommendations. The government has recently taken steps to encourage inbound student mobility through streamlining the visa process and allowing for students to receive multi-entry visas when engaging in long-term courses. In May 2009, universities were directed to increase information and support for international students, through launching websites, and by providing orientation sessions and increasing monitoring services for students while in country. Further, the government has planned to establish five universities that specifically target Indian diaspora students with plans to reserve half of the admission spots specifically for them. The first of these institutions is planned to be a collaborative effort between the government and the Manipal Group, to commence in 2010.

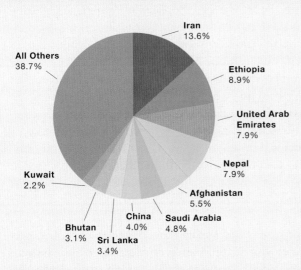

57

REGION:
Asia
COUNTRY:
India

Figure 6: Places of Origin of International Students in India, 2008/09

Source: AIU

The Foreign Educational Institutions (Regulation of Entry and Operations) Bill 2010 will further open the educational landscape to partnerships and collaborative arrangements with foreign providers. The bill aims to remove a number of prior requirements for educational partnerships as well as some of the more debated proposals that delayed its passage over the past three years. With the elimination of a prior requirement that foreign providers partner directly with Indian institutions, both providers and higher education institutions stand to benefit from this policy change. A reduction in bureaucratic procedures will allow providers to gain access to a new market of non-mobile Indian students, while the educational infrastructure in India will be strengthened through foreign investments. The bill will eliminate the condition that prevents foreign institutions from conferring degrees, allowing Indian students to receive credentials from expectedly well-known and high-quality institutions without the necessity of going abroad.

This bill (currently still pending legislative approval) has the potential to be a significant boon to the internationalization of Indian higher education,

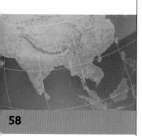

as the linkages built between foreign institutions and India could lead to increased teacher and researcher exchange, as well as an increase in international students. Given the regulatory complications experienced during prior branching attempts of certain prominent foreign institutions (such as Carnegie Mellon University and Illinois Institute of Technology) that led to their subsequent closures, it remains to be seen which institutions may move forward with the development of Indian branches. The easing of a number of the previous restrictions under the bill should result in a friendlier environment for this international collaboration. The "brand name" that top international institutions would offer would attract students from home countries that are interested in an international exchange with the familiarity of a known provider, as well as students from other countries who seek out the cache of the foreign institution but are also attracted to the appeal of India as a destination.

In an effort to internationalize higher education, a number of Indian institutions, mostly private, have set up branch campuses abroad, mainly in Southeast Asia and the Middle East. Indian HEIs now have programs in Singapore, Dubai and Malaysia, and plan to expand to other destinations to host larger numbers of Indian students in regional education hubs throughout the world. These branch campuses also cater to the local student population in the host countries.

The Role of Universities and Higher Education Associations
In collaboration with UGC, the Association of Indian Universities (AIU) sets and implements national policies related to tertiary education, acting as a liaison amongst universities and between HEIs and the Government. AIU also advocates for increasing standards of instruction and education quality and collects education data. Assessing the scope of international student mobility in India remains a particular challenge given the porous borders that India shares with its neighboring countries, including Bangladesh, Bhutan and Nepal. In addition to data collection, AIU supports the internationalization efforts of the higher education system in a variety of direct and indirect ways, particularly in the areas of quality assessment, information sharing and student talent identification.

AIU has been instrumental in signing Memorandums of Understanding (MOUs) with other countries to support inbound mobility, which allow for a reciprocal recognition of degrees awarded by accredited institutions.

- Approximately 268,000 Indian students studied abroad in 2008.

- There were over 21,000 international students in India in 2008/09.

- The top five places of origin in 2008/09 were Iran, Ethiopia, United Arab Emirates, Nepal and Afghanistan.

Source: AIU

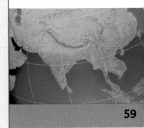

59

REGION:
Asia
COUNTRY:
India

AIU has signed these MOUs with Australia, Egypt, Germany, Russia and Sri Lanka. Quality recognition can be a significant challenge for students seeking admission into institutions abroad, so this facet of AIU's operations removes a considerable barrier to mobility for Indian students and students from countries with reciprocal degree recognition MOUs with India.

To facilitate outbound mobility and support the strengthening of research capacity in the country, AIU coordinates National Research Conventions, which link international host institutions with promising young Indian students interested in pursuing research careers. The objectives of these conventions are to identify students with research promise, while simultaneously promoting the need for talented researchers in the country. Students selected through these conventions are potentially eligible for research fellowships at universities in countries such as Canada, Germany and the Netherlands.

AIU's work also includes publication, and the *Universities Handbook* provides pertinent details about accreditation status, course offering, admissions procedures, faculty information and affiliation of its current members (365) including three associate members: Kathmandu University (Nepal), University of Mauritius, and the Royal University of Bhutan.

Other higher education initiatives in India have also created platforms for collaboration between local and international partners in higher education. The Indo-American Chamber of Commerce (IACC) facilitates the Indo-American Education Forum, to support the expansion of the private sector in higher education and to create more international linkages between Indian and international higher education institutions. The Emerging Directions

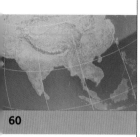

in Global Education (EDGE) forum, launched in 2007, convenes annually and brings together global leaders in education to address the most pressing issues in internationalization and to facilitate knowledge exchange. EDGE also works with partner organizations on research and publication on higher education in India.

Progressive educational policies of recent years to internationalize India's higher education sector, set by the government and carried out by institutions such as AIU, IACC, and EDGE, are likely to increase the international student population and begin the significant task of reducing the inbound-outbound mobility gap. As evidenced by its large mobile student population, growing economy and increasing middle class, India remains crucial to the discussions surrounding global student mobility.

---

[1] Along with information from the Association of Indian Universities (AIU), this section is adapted from *International India: A Turning Point in Educational Exchange with the U.S.*, edited by Rajika Bhandari (2010).

REGION: **Asia**

COUNTRY: **Japan**

By Japan Student Services Organization (JASSO)

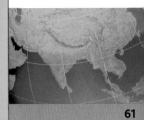

Despite demographic shifts that have resulted in reduced numbers of Japanese students pursuing education abroad in recent years, the government is keenly interested in increasing student mobility. In an effort to develop its higher education system as a hub for global international students and to support the exchange of students, particularly within the region, the government has recently implemented key initiatives to support both inbound and outbound student mobility.

Through the framework of the "300,000 International Students Plan" announced in July 2009, the government has sought to increase Japan's international student population to 300,000 students by 2020 through a series of measures by:

- Expanding information resources about Japan and its higher education system.
- Encouraging internationalization of higher education institutions.
- Strengthening support services for international students.

The first component of the plan outlines a proactive, coordinated dissemination of information about Japanese culture and higher education to increase interest in Japan as a destination. Key stakeholders abroad such as Japan's consulates, embassies and branch campuses of universities are encouraged to work collaboratively to provide comprehensive information on studying in Japan to potential international students. This measure also includes increasing the number of language education bases to promote Japanese language acquisition abroad.

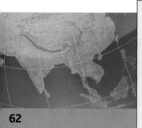

REGION:
Asia
COUNTRY:
Japan

The Japanese 300,000 Plan

- Calls for 300,000 international students by 2020, up from the 2009/10 total of 132,000.

- Establishes core "Global 30" universities with funding to internationalize at home and abroad through global offices.

- JASSO, an administrative agency under MEXT, helps implement this policy by overseeing national scholarship programs and student services.

A second component of the plan focuses on streamlining various processes for international students to ease their entry into the country, from the initial application process, to visa and immigration protocol to enrollment. The plan calls for institutions to better inform potential students about Japanese admissions requirements, particularly in areas related to required entrance exams. The plan also aims to improve the standard admission test for non-Japanese students, the Examination for Japanese University Admission for International Students (EJU).

As the third major component of the plan, the Ministry of Education, Culture, Sports, Science and Technology (MEXT) launched the "Project for Establishing Core Universities for Internationalization (Global 30)."[1] Of thirty total Japanese universities proposed in the plan, thirteen have been selected thus far to participate as core educational centers charged with increasing the number of both inbound and outbound students. These universities will set out to accomplish this by focusing efforts on:

- Revising admissions processes.
- Establishing overseas offices to bolster recruitment efforts.
- Facilitating Fall admissions.
- Increasing the number of degree programs and courses offered solely in English, while also providing opportunities for Japanese language and cultural instruction.
- And increasing the number of foreign teachers in particular courses.

To support these internationalization goals, the selected institutions will receive increased governmental funding with the expectation of recruiting 3,000 to 8,000 international students each over a five-year period. In addition, the government has strategically selected seven countries for establishing international offices in order to communicate information to potential international students. These offices, affiliated with one of the "Global 30" universities, will be located in the following cities and will serve as the liaison for the Study in Japan initiative:

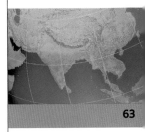

- Bonn, Germany (Waseda University)

- Cairo, Egypt (Kyushu University)

- Hanoi, Vietnam (Kyoto University)

- Hyderabad, India (The University of Tokyo)

- Moscow and Novosibirsk, Russia (Tohoku University)

- New Delhi, India (Ritsumeikan University)

- Tashkent, Uzbekistan (Nagoya University)

- Tunis, Tunisia (University of Tsukuba)

The fourth component of the plan centers on improving support services for international students within the higher education system. A primary focus is on housing and increasing the options available to international students through building more dormitories and providing assistance with securing off-campus housing. Other forms of support targeted at self-funded international students include governmental and merit-based scholarships, in addition to financial counseling services.

The final measure of the plan involves the integration of international students into Japanese society after completion of their studies through employment. The government, universities and private industry have been directed to increase international students' job prospects through specific measures. Universities have been instructed to improve career service offerings, while the government would consider possible immigration reforms to extend the duration of stay for international students after completion of academic requirements. Further, companies have been encouraged to develop policies to accept international graduates as candidates for employment. Through these measures, it is expected that further internationalization of the higher education system will also yield an increasingly internationalized work force in Japan.

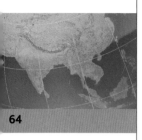

64

Regional Cooperation and Exchange

Beyond the "300,000 International Students Plan" and associated "Global 30" plan, a commitment to fostering exchange partnerships within the region was reinforced at the October 2009 meeting of the heads of the People's Republic of China, Japan, and the Republic of Korea. This meeting commemorated the tenth anniversary of the original trilateral cooperation agreement between these countries and focused more specifically on developing youth and university exchanges. The then Japanese Prime Minister Yukio Hatoyama proposed further intra-governmental efforts aimed at quality assurance issues, and the implementation of a regional credit transfer system as well as formal exchange programs.

In April 2010, the resulting "Japan-China-Korea Committee for Promoting Exchange and Cooperation among Universities" met in Tokyo to build upon these ideas. The "CAMPUS Asia" project was subsequently created, which aims to develop concrete approaches to quality assurance issues of credit transfer, grading policies and university evaluation among the countries to foster increased intra-regional student mobility. This committee has agreed to hold tri-annual meetings.

Scholarship and Program Administration

In support of these national initiatives and policies, the Japan Student Services Organization (JASSO) provides services to students and higher education institutions to support student mobility. JASSO serves as an informational resource for prospective international students and Japanese students interested in studying abroad. It also organizes education fairs overseas, as well as college guidance fairs and study abroad fairs in Japan.

JASSO administers scholarship programs and provides financial support services for both domestic and international higher education students. Through the Student Exchange Support Program, scholarships are granted to both inbound and outbound short-term exchange students, as well as to Japanese students seeking long-term and degree programs abroad. JASSO is one of the administrative agencies that manages a prominent national exchange program, the Japan-East Asia Network of Exchange for Students and Youths (JENESYS), which was established by the government in 2007 to provide a variety of exchange opportunities for students from the region to visit Japan, thereby promoting mutual understanding and fostering positive regard for Japan among the youth of Asia.

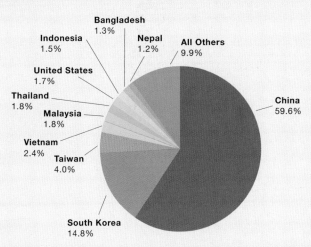

Figure 7: Places of Origin of International Students in Japan, 2009

(Source: JASSO)

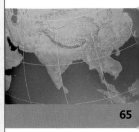

REGION:
Asia
COUNTRY:
Japan

JASSO provides student services to international students, from the initial stages of admission to Japanese universities through their enrollment in academic programs and as alumni. In addition, the organization is primarily responsible for:

- Facilitating the Examination for Japanese University Admission for International Students (EJU).

- Providing Japanese language education for students interested in higher education in Japan.

- Managing international houses, supporting the construction of accommodations, and assisting universities in leasing accommodations for these students.

- Providing follow-up services for former international students in Japan to support their continued academic endeavors and employment prospects.

Through follow-up research guidance, fellowships, and job hunting seminars, students also receive assistance in pursuing further academic and career opportunities. An email newsletter, the "Japan Alumni eNews," allows

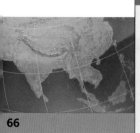

66

REGION:
Asia

COUNTRY:
Japan

facts and figures

- There were over 132,000 international students enrolled in Japanese HEIs as of May 1, 2009.

- The top five places of origin as of May 2009 were China, South Korea, Taiwan, Vietnam and Malaysia.

- There was an overall seven percent increase in the number of international students during the 2009 academic year.

(Source: JASSO)

former international students to network and keeps them connected to their educational experience in Japan.

Through articulated national policies such as the "300,000 International Students Plan" and the "Global 30," Japan has positioned itself to become an educational hub for the world's mobile student population. The government's leadership to encourage exchange among neighboring nations is an important step in promoting positive relations and cooperation within the region. The work of JASSO and other key organizations in Japan to strengthen the systems outlined in these policies is crucial for ensuring a seamless transition for international students to gain entry to Japanese higher education institutions, focus on their studies through well-coordinated student support services, obtain a high quality education and ultimately become individual ambassadors for Japan.

Japan Student Services Organization (JASSO): JASSO manages a wide-range of support programs for Japanese students as well as international students in an integrated manner.

---

[1] This project is under review and is contingent upon continued funding.

REGION: **Europe**

Along with the United States, several European countries are the top destinations for the world's globally mobile students. These include the United
Kingdom, hosting 13 percent of all mobile students worldwide, France (eight
percent) and Germany (seven percent). Included in these percentages are the
European students who remain in Europe but study outside of their home
country. These students comprise the largest share of international students
in European higher education. When studying abroad, approximately 77
percent of mobile students from Western European choose host destinations
within Western Europe.

The Bologna Process, initiated in 1999 to create a common area for higher
education in Europe, has accelerated the process of internationalization across
the region. A major goal of the Bologna Process is to increase access to the
European Higher Education Area (EHEA) by harmonizing the degree structure and to make Europe more appealing for inter- and intra-regional student
mobility. Although mobility levels have not reached the expected high levels
predicted at the signing of the Bologna Declaration, as a region Europe today
has the highest market share of mobile students in the world, totaling nearly
48 percent (UNESCO, 2010).

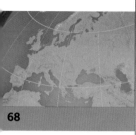

As a sending region, Europe's share of international students is 26 percent of the world total (UNESCO, 2010). In 2008, the outbound mobility ratio for Western Europe was nearly three percent with the following countries seeing particularly high ratios: Cyprus (93 percent), Iceland (15 percent), Ireland (ten percent), Norway (six percent) and Switzerland (five percent). In contrast, less than two percent of tertiary students from Italy, the Netherlands, Spain and the United Kingdom studied outside of their home country. In Central and Eastern Europe, about 1.6 percent of tertiary students study abroad, with Russian students being the least mobile and students from Slovakia the most mobile. Russia and the Czech Republic attract the largest number of Central and Eastern European students moving within Central and Eastern Europe.

Some European countries are prioritizing the retention of local talent, while others have set goals to continue to internationalize universities by recruiting students from Europe and other regions. Two flagship initiatives that have contributed to Europe's position as a leading region for hosting international students are the ERASMUS and the Erasmus Mundus Programs, funded by the European Commission. The programs provide scholarships for students from European and non-European nations to study in European universities. The European Commission also promotes mobility of research scholars and university linkages, and it recently launched the *Youth on the Move* initiative, to foster more educational exchange in the region.

European universities have also taken independent action to make their academic programs more attractive to international students. There are numerous inter-regional schemes and joint-degree programs that have been established through partnerships around the world. Some foreign universities have branch campuses in Europe, and in turn, European universities have a significant presence abroad.   In addition to offering standard Master's degrees, many universities in countries where English is not the official language now offer one year Master's programs taught in English. As of 2010, there were over 4,000 English-language Master's programs offered in non-Anglophone Europe, with Germany in the lead, offering over 100 Master's degree programs in English. This has become a particularly popular trend for business, economics and engineering degrees, which attract a large number of students from Asia, and increasingly from other regions. European doctoral degrees are also being promoted internationally to attract top researchers from around the world.

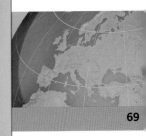

Promoting mobility and exchange in Finland reflects broad national motivations centered on creating an international environment for higher education in Finland, providing students with international skills and with better resources for working life, and understanding different cultures. Internationalization also benefits industry, strengthens the quality and capacity of higher education and research, and helps build capacity and development in other countries.

Finland actively participates in both European Union mobility programs (such as ERASMUS) and Nordic Mobility Programs funded by the Nordic Council of Ministers. Through these programs, most mobility occurs between Finland and other European Union (EU), Nordic and Baltic countries. Russia is another important national priority for exchange, and national funds are directed specifically toward mobility between Finland and Russia.

One example of this collaboration is the Finnish-Russian Student and Teacher Exchange (FIRST) Program, which supports cooperation between Finnish and Russian higher education institutions. As another priority, the Finnish government also directs funding toward mobility programs with Asian countries, in particular China, India, Japan, and South Korea. For example, in April 2009, the Centre for International Mobility (CIMO) opened its first overseas higher education and research support office in China. The office, located in Shanghai, assists Finnish higher education institutions in making contacts with local institutions and promoting Finnish higher education in China.

70

REGION:
Europe
COUNTRY:
Finland

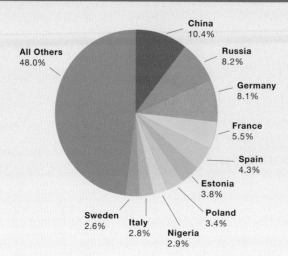

All Others
48.0%

China
10.4%

Russia
8.2%

Germany
8.1%

France
5.5%

Spain
4.3%

Estonia
3.8%

Poland
3.4%

Sweden
2.6%

Italy
2.8%

Nigeria
2.9%

Figure 8: Places of Origin of International Students in Finland, 2009

Source: CIMO

Internationalizing education and increasing student mobility are relatively high on the political agenda in Finland. In 2009, the Finnish Ministry of Education published its *Strategy for the Internationalization of Higher Education Institutions in Finland 2009-2015.* It aims to create an internationally strong and attractive higher education institution and research community in Finland that promotes society's ability to function in an open international environment. The five aims outlined for the internationalization of Finnish higher education are:

- Supporting an international higher education community that provides competencies to work in an international environment
- Increasing quality and attractiveness of Finnish institutions
- Promoting the export of expertise
- Supporting a multicultural society
- Promoting global responsibility.

The strategy also establishes detailed mobility benchmarks that institutions will aim to meet. These targets include increasing the study abroad participation rate among Finnish higher education students to reach eight percent of all students in universities of applied sciences and six percent of all students in universities, while ensuring an equal number of international students studying abroad in Finnish institutions. The Internationalization Strategy also includes a seven percent target goal for inbound international students in full-degree programs.

With the signing of the Leuven Communiqué in 2009, the Finnish Ministry of Education, along with other Ministries comprising the European Higher Education Area (EHEA), set a target that 20 percent of all students should graduate with an international experience abroad by 2020.

CIMO administers several EU, Nordic, and national mobility programs in Finland on behalf of the Finnish Ministry and the EU, while cooperating with other agencies and institutions to promote mobility.

Examples of nationally funded programs that CIMO administers include:

■ FIRST Program: supports cooperation of Finnish and Russian higher education institutions.

■ CIMO Fellowships: scholarships for young researchers and university teaching staff to conduct research or teach in Finland.

■ North-South-South Higher Education Institution Network Program and Higher Education Institution Institutional Cooperation Instrument (HEI ICI): these programs fund institutional cooperation between Finland and developing countries.

71

REGION:
Europe
COUNTRY:
Finland

facts and figures

■ In 2008/09, there were over 21,000 international students studying in Finland.[1]

■ The top five places of origin in 2009 were China, Russia, Germany, France and Spain.

■ The Centre for International Mobility (CIMO) operates under the Finnish Ministry of Education and administers several mobility programs in Finland.

Source: CIMO

■ Trainee Exchange: CIMO, in collaboration with partner organizations, arranges placements in recipient countries including those in Asia, South America, Russia and others.

The Academy of Finland is the prime funding agency for basic research in Finland. The Academy of Finland is also committed to promoting the internationalization of Finnish science and research. It provides funding to support the international cooperation of research centers and teams and supports the mobility of researchers.

This multilateral cooperation within the framework of the Bologna Process facilitates mobility in and outside the Nordic region. One example of cooperation with Russia, for example, is the Cross-Border University, a university consortium of four Finnish and five Russian institutions.

Centre for International Mobility (CIMO): The Centre for International Mobility (CIMO), operating under the Finnish Ministry of Education, administers several EU, Nordic and national mobility programs in Finland on behalf of the Finnish Ministry and EU. In addition to its main areas of program administration, CIMO publishes mobility-related publications and promotional materials, and conducts studies on topics relevant to the internationalization of education, such as its *Fact and Figures* report series. It recently also undertook a study on degree programs taught through a foreign language in Finnish higher education. CIMO is also responsible for the data collection of international student exchanges to and from Finland. These data are published annually on CIMO's web site.

---

[1] This figure combines the number of incoming exchange students counted by CIMO, in addition to foreign degree students based on Statistics Finland data. When these categories are disaggregated, the countries of origin vary: exchange students tend to come mainly from EU countries, whereas degree students tend to come from Asia, Russia and Africa.

REGION: **Europe**

COUNTRY: **France**

By CampusFrance

The French government has enacted various policies to guide the internationalization of higher education, promoting diplomacy as "soft power" through the relationships developed between the citizens of France and of other countries. In terms of broad national aims, the country also looks to promote the French language abroad and the impact of international students in the French higher education sector.

Recognizing higher education as a public good, the French government defrays a large share of the overall cost of higher education by heavily subsidizing study programs. On average, 10,150€ per student per year is invested by the French government, substantially reducing students' tuition costs. Financial gain through high tuition fees is not an objective of the French government. International students benefit from the same low fees and other social advantages as domestic students. Additional benefits extended to all students in the French higher education system include a network of student facilities and services, such as university housing, rent subsidies, health insurance, student clubs and associations, and discounts on public transportation and cultural events.

When CampusFrance, the national agency for the promotion of French higher education, was created in 1998 under the former name of "EduFrance," the government designated Asia and Latin America as key target regions for attracting international students. Since that time, however, the regional scope has expanded to include the Middle East, Africa and other European countries; promotional activities are now implemented throughout the world.

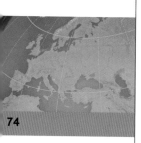

REGION:
Europe
COUNTRY:
France

Other national bodies are also responsible for supporting international students in France. Égide is an organization involved in providing services to students. For over 45 years, Égide has been managing international exchange and grant programs for international students and interns taking part in courses in France or abroad. At the head of the national network of the *Centre régional des oeuvres universitaires et scolaires* (CNOUS), the *Centre national des oeuvres universitaires et scolaires* is an independent public establishment that manages a network of student social services domestically and internationally. Supporting a national policy of equal opportunity and access to higher education, CNOUS provides assistance in student services, from housing, grants and social and cultural activities, to administering international mobility programs and partnerships.

As a result of the merger of CampusFrance and Égide, a new agency called Campus France will be created in early 2011. The international sector of CNOUS is due to join the organization by the end of 2011. The new structure will be under the joint supervision of the Ministries of Foreign and European Affairs and Higher Education and Research. It will have the status of a public institution (*Etablissement public à caractère industriel et commercial*) and will be responsible for the promotion of French higher education, hosting services for foreign students and researchers, the management of scholarship programs and the promotion and development of higher education delivered via new technologies.

A new system of research and higher education clusters *Pôles de recherche et d'enseignement supérieur* (PRES) adopted by law in April 2006 encourages higher education institutions in a region or city to share resources that enhance international visibility and reputation. The PRES member institutions collaborate on activities linked to doctoral studies, research, exchange with the private sector, and international relations. The PRES is increasingly developing activities in the field of international student services. The *Opération Campus* program, another government-supported initiative, aims to improve services offered to international students, largely through renovation of university facilities through massive state investment.

The Role of CampusFrance
CampusFrance (renamed as such in 2007) is a national agency under the supervision of several ministries and is responsible for the promotion of French

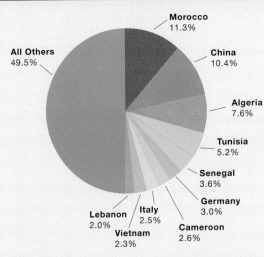

Morocco 11.3%

All Others 49.5%

China 10.4%

Algeria 7.6%

Tunisia 5.2%

Senegal 3.6%

Germany 3.0%

Cameroon 2.6%

Italy 2.5%

Vietnam 2.3%

Lebanon 2.0%

Figure 9: Places of Origin of International Students in France, 2009/10

(Source: CampusFrance)

75

REGION:
Europe
COUNTRY:
France

higher education abroad. Under the supervision of these ministerial author-ities and in conjunction with higher education institutions and their official conferences, CampusFrance aims to:

- Promote French higher education programs throughout the world.
- Offer international students a path to success via higher education in France.
- Assist international students at all stages, from initial inquiry to their actual stay in France and concluding with the trip home to their countries of origin.
- In association with higher education institutions, the PRES, the French ministries as well as Égide and the CNOUS, CampusFrance is working towards the improvement of international student services in France.

Since the creation of the agency, the number of international students in France has increased dramatically, from 160,533 in 1999/00 to 278,213 in 2009/10.[1]

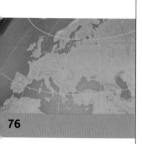

CampusFrance works under the supervision of the Ministries of Foreign and European Affairs, Higher Education and Research and Immigration, Integration, National Identity and Co-Development. It carries out its activities in conjunction with French higher education institutions and their official conferences. The agency has 242 member organizations, including *Grandes Ecoles*, business schools, engineering schools, specialized institutions and most universities.

CampusFrance has a network of 116 overseas offices and 24 annexes in 89 countries placed under the supervision of the French Embassy in each country. These offices provide counseling and information services to individual students interested in pursuing their studies in France, while promoting French higher education at local institutions. Overseas, CampusFrance staff also accompany students through the administrative and consular processes prior to their arrival in France. An online application system that can also handle visa request procedures has been set up in close to 30 countries.

CampusFrance organizes a number of promotional events throughout the world each year, which attract on average a total of 160,000 visitors. The program of events, in which representatives of French HEIs take part, includes higher education fairs, thematic university tours, specialized networking sessions, conferences, workshops on academic innovation, and the promotion of doctoral programs.

CampusFrance manages a comprehensive online catalogue with a multi-criteria search engine, containing over 36,000 study programs and information on doctoral programs, research units and partner laboratories on its multilingual website: www.campusfrance.org. Furthermore, more than 50 country-specific websites in 27 languages have also been developed. In addition, CampusFrance has developed a scholarship database which includes details of nearly 600 scholarship programs for international students coming to France.

CampusFrance regularly publishes multimedia information guides designed for international students, including an annual catalogue of 600 programs taught in English and a general guide to studying and living in France. It also produces regular publications, such as studies, analyses and newsletters aimed at its members, higher education institutions, and many other institutional bodies, in order to raise awareness about mobility and internationalization issues.

Regional Promotion and Collaboration

By promoting French higher education through activities jointly organized with other countries, CampusFrance and other French institutions are able to take part in more large-scale events, ensure a presence in countries where they are underrepresented, exchange best practices with partner countries, benefit from increased cost-effectiveness, and enjoy increased visibility. France is traditionally associated with being at the heart of Europe. This image is reinforced by France taking part in fairs under the European banner, which promotes the excellence of European higher education.

Along with other European Union Member States, notably Germany and the Netherlands, CampusFrance has funded and launched with partner organizations education fairs in Asia and Latin America. The agency has also been involved in European Commission initiatives for the promotion of European Higher Education. For example, it was the lead organization of a consortium composed of the British Council, DAAD and Nuffic for the organization of European Higher Education Fairs, symposia and match-making activities in seven Asian countries. These events, bringing together institutions and national agencies from all 27 EU Member States, reached a combined audience of over 100,000 visitors.

77

REGION:
Europe
COUNTRY:
France

facts and figures

- In 2009/10, there were over 278,000 international students in higher education in France.

- The top five places of origin in 2009/10 were Morocco, China, Algeria, Tunisia and Senegal.

- CampusFrance is the national agency for promoting French higher education abroad.

Source: CampusFrance

78

As a way of building capacity, sharing information and influencing policy, CampusFrance produces various studies and reports on international student mobility, based on data provided by the French Ministry of Higher Education and Research (MSER/DGSIP/DGRI/SIES/DEPP), and international sources such as UNESCO and the European Commission. One important annual publication of CampusFrance, *International Student Mobility: Key Figures*, provides an overview of worldwide mobility tendencies, including data on the major destination countries for international students. Other publications, which are often linked to on-going CampusFrance activities, focus on incoming student mobility to France from specific geographical regions or countries. A paper on international students from the Maghreb and Africa was recently published in conjunction with a training session for CampusFrance staff in this region. These and other publications provide an overview of global mobility trends, as well as data and analyses focusing on incoming student mobility within France. Diffused widely, CampusFrance publications constitute a useful resource for all specialists involved in student mobility.

CampusFrance: Under the oversight of the French government and in close cooperation with institutions of higher education and their associations, CampusFrance promotes French higher education programs throughout the world, offering international students a pathway to success through postsecondary study in France. CampusFrance's role extends from home country to host country and from answering prospective students' first inquiries right down to helping them plan their stay in France and their return home.

---

[1] Source: Ministère de l'Education nationale/ Ministère de l'Enseignement supérieur et de la Recherche : Repères et références statistiques sur les enseignements, la formation et la recherche, Paris, 2010.

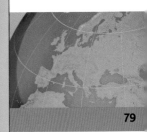

79

Germany is an important hub for global student mobility—it is not only a leading destination for international students, but also a large source of students who study abroad. The German government aims to promote student mobility within its broader strategy for the internationalization of science and research, *Strategie der Bundesregierung zur Internationalisierung von Wissenschaft und Forschung* (Federal Government's Internationalization Strategy for Science and Research). Adopted in February 2008, this strategy outlines four main goals to approach the challenges that global competition poses to Germany's science and innovation system.

Two of these goals have direct implications on Germany's mobility efforts: to strengthen research collaboration with global leaders and to increase long-term cooperation with developing countries in education, research and development. A number of policy measures to achieve these goals have also been outlined within the strategy, namely coordinating and bolstering Germany's research presence abroad, analyzing international trends in research and innovation and promoting Germany as a hub for research and development in key target countries.

There are various entities responsible for the implementation of these policies, such as the German Academic Exchange Service (DAAD), the German Research Foundation (DFG—Deutsche Forschungsgemeinschaft), the Alexander von Humboldt-Foundation (AvH—Alexander von Humboldt-Stiftung) and—last, but not least—the universities themselves. The joint efforts of these stakeholders to support this strategy have resulted

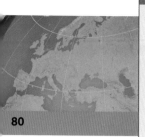

facts and figures

- In 2009/10, Germany hosted over 244,000 international students.

- The top five places of origin in 2009/10 were China, Turkey, Russia, Poland and Ukraine.

- The top destinations for German students are Netherlands, Austria and United Kingdom.

- The annual statistical publication on inbound and outbound student mobility is published by the German Academic Exchange Service (DAAD).

Source: DAAD

in Germany ranking fourth among the host countries of all globally mobile students (roughly 244,000 foreign students in 2010). Additionally, there were over 90,300 German students who studied abroad.

Immigration policies and laws have improved within Germany to support its appeal as an attractive destination for international students. For example, the option to remain in Germany after graduation in order to find employment has been extended. Non-EU citizens who graduate from a German university can extend their stay for up to one year in order to find and accept a job.

Further, a legislative initiative ("Visawarndateierrichtungsgesetz"), which would have led to stricter visa regulations for individuals or institutions inviting international students and scholars from other countries, was abandoned before entering parliament. The DAAD and other institutions contributed to the decision through advocacy efforts to the Ministry responsible for the legislation.

The Role of the DAAD in Educational Mobility
As a key goal, by supporting students and academics from abroad in order to create lifelong friends of Germany, the DAAD implements programs that target future leaders in education, science and research, culture, industry and commerce, politics, and the media. The DAAD also supports German students and academics abroad, recognizing their potential as future and cosmopolitan leaders who have international and intercultural experience.

Furthermore, its goals for student mobility extend toward development and capacity-building areas in other countries in support of their economic and democratic reform processes.

Largely funded by various federal Ministries, the DAAD cooperates with the government in developing new scholarship programs in order to reach student mobility goals and targets. The DAAD also cooperates with foreign governments, for example, by negotiating agreements on co-financed scholarship and exchange programs.

As the DAAD is a self-administered organization of Germany's higher education institutions, many institutions are members of the DAAD with voting rights to influence the management and constitution of the organization (e.g., through elections of decision-making bodies, statute resolutions, etc.) as well as the basic principles and policies underlying the development and design of programs. Representatives from the universities regularly meet and provide input on decision-making to the DAAD; the institutions are also authorized to apply for DAAD-administered

facts and figures

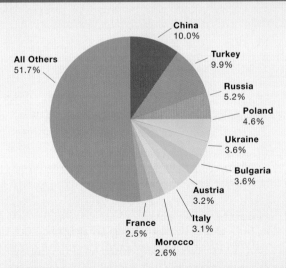

China
10.0%

Turkey
9.9%

Russia
5.2%

Poland
4.6%

Ukraine
3.6%

Bulgaria
3.6%

Austria
3.2%

Italy
3.1%

Morocco
2.6%

France
2.5%

All Others
51.7%

Figure 10: Places of Origin of International Students in Germany, 2009/10

Source: DAAD

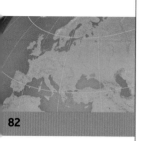

programs. Through this ongoing exchange and dialogue, the DAAD member institutions collaborate in multiple ways to increase and enhance student mobility.

The DAAD also cooperates with other large education associations as partners in promoting student mobility. Activities involve close collaboration with the DFG and AvH, the German Rectors' Conference (HRK, or *Hochschulrektorenkonferenz*) and the Standing Conference of the Ministers of Education (KMK, or *Kultusministerkonferenz*). Along with the DAAD, these organizations serve as members of the "Alliance" of leading German education and research associations. The Alliance acts as a counselor for the German government in the policy field of science and academic education, and on important issues of student mobility.

The DAAD's contribution to promoting student mobility in Germany is quite diverse and includes offering a broad range of approximately 250 funding programs for international and German applicants and institutions. Scholarship programs available include undergraduate, postgraduate and doctoral programs, study visits, specialist courses, internships, research placement stays, lectureships, project works, university partnership programs, degree programs and creating efficient university structures. The majority of programs administered by the DAAD target individual applicants.

Among the most popular and well-established programs open to applicants from all over the world are:
- Study Scholarships for Graduates of All Disciplines
- Research Grants for Doctoral Candidates and Young Academics and Scientists
- Research Stays for University Academics and Scientists
- Berlin Artists-in-Residence Program.

An increasing number of programs are also directed toward institutions such as universities. Promoted by the DAAD, these programs are aimed at internationalizing institutions and they take the form of double-degree programs or improving mentoring for international students. Recently, the DAAD set up a new mobility program, which offers universities the possibility to apply for funding for scholarships that can be given by universities to their students. The aim is to give more students the opportunity to study abroad and to allow the institution to decide what form the scholarship will take—such as one supporting an internship, semester stay, or a short-term doctoral stay, etc.—according to the HEIs' individual internationalization strategy.

In addition to program administration and collaboration among government, other like-minded organizations and higher education institutions, the DAAD also engages in research to gauge the effectiveness of its programs, conducting mobility research in Germany through its annual statistical publication, *Wissenschaft Weltoffen*. Other ongoing studies have addressed the level of internationalization of German higher education institutions, which may help universities improve their own efforts in increasing student mobility.

German Academic Exchange Service (DAAD): The German Academic Exchange Service (DAAD) is the German national agency for the support of international academic cooperation. The DAAD is a publicly-funded independent organization of higher education institutions in Germany.

83

REGION:
Europe
COUNTRY:
Germany

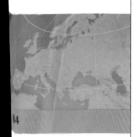

84

REGION: **Europe**

COUNTRY: **Ireland**

By Education Ireland

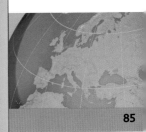

85

REGION:
Europe
COUNTRY:
Ireland

Governance and Structure of Internationalization

The internationalization of higher education in Ireland has been progressing steadily over the last 20 years with an average of ten percent of the student population domiciled outside the country. This has been achieved in spite of relatively low levels of government involvement and incomplete strategies and structures at the national level. This situation has changed fundamentally in the recent past with the formation in 2009 of a high-level group of key players in international education (government departments and agencies as well as higher education institutions) to develop an international education strategy and action plan for 2010-2015.

The Group, which issued its final report in Autumn 2010, believes that there is potential for substantive growth in international education in Ireland and this can contribute significantly to the Irish economy. However, there is a deep understanding of the problems associated with placing economic rationale ahead of other equally important factors in developing international education.

The main goal at the national level is to nurture future global relationships, thus requiring Ireland to offer high quality education and an outstanding experience to international students. Therefore, growth will take place only in tandem with the full development of necessary supports to ensure a quality experience at all levels. Large-scale projects aimed at short-term rapid growth and mass recruitment will not be a characteristic of the internationalization of Irish education. Rather Ireland will present a more "niche" offering of a

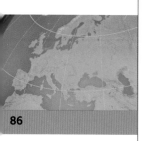

high quality education that is strongly integrated with domestic students, which will offer an unparalleled experience to students and add significant value to the career outcomes of all students who study in Ireland.

Success in this environment will require the development of long-term and sustainable processes and structures, based on high-quality, holistic and balanced engagement with international partners. While Irish education is already very outwardly-focused, this strategy will precipitate the facilitation of greater outward mobility, and foster the international experience of Irish staff and students, which will widen and deepen collaboration and research-based linkages and internationalize curricula for Irish institutions. This will help to further develop Irish involvement in trans-national education, emphasizing the delivery of Irish academic programs overseas, as well as establishing links with institutions outside of Ireland, which can continue to engage Ireland in multilateral initiatives such as the Bologna Process.

Historically, Ireland has had very strong links with developing countries, especially in education. Ireland is positioned to play an important role in the capacity building of research and educational facilities, which, in turn, is crucial to scientific development and the growth of civil society in those countries. Such activities are consistent with Ireland's overall approach to development and education issues and represent an investment in future relationships.

The educational interests of Ireland's international students, their safety and security, their integration with the wider student body and their overall experience of Ireland are central to the country's approach. Policies and strategies will be developed to ensure that students have a positive experience at all stages, from application to graduation, and beyond.

The Current Situation
Ireland is committed to a collaborative approach to internationalization and the new "shared vision," which will bring a number of agencies who are currently involved in the development of international education closer together.

In terms of structure, the promotion of the national brand, "Education Ireland" is, and will continue to be managed by Enterprise Ireland, while the National Qualifications Authority will focus its activities in this sphere on quality, accreditation and welfare issues; the Higher Education Authority

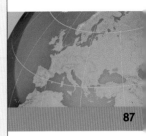

■ There were over 25,000 international students in Ireland in 2009/10.

■ The top places of origin in 2009/10 were the United States, China, France, UK and Northern Ireland and Germany.

■ The Higher Level Group is comprised of government departments, Irish agencies and HEIs, and aims to address the internationalization of higher education in Ireland.

Source: Education Ireland

REGION:
Europe
COUNTRY:
Ireland

and Department of Education and Skills oversee policy areas. The activities will be overseen and guided by the expert group which is chaired by the Department of Education and Skills.

Education Ireland is managed by Enterprise Ireland (EI), the Irish government agency responsible for the development and promotion of the business sector. EI's mission is to accelerate the development of world-class Irish companies to achieve strong positions in global markets, resulting in increased national and regional prosperity.

Education Ireland promotes Ireland as a destination for a high quality education and provides comprehensive information on studying in Ireland for prospective students through its website, social media sites and electronic and printed materials. Education Ireland also coordinates the activities of member institutions internationally; activities include the organization and management of education fairs and conferences overseas, market intelligence, market coordination, strategy development, training and the collection of statistics on international students in Ireland (http://tinyurl.com/347zk2s).

The Irish government also promotes study abroad among Irish students in higher education and all Irish higher education institutions (HEIs) are involved with the European Union ERASMUS programs and other international exchange programs. Ireland's motivation here is driven largely by goals to expand student horizons in terms of current education and future employment, develop and expand links with international higher education

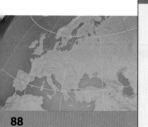

88

REGION:
Europe
COUNTRY:
Ireland

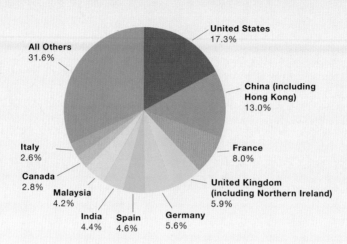

Figure 11: Places of Origin of International Students in Ireland, 2009/10

(Source: Education Ireland)

institutions, and deepen international knowledge of the Irish education system. As mentioned above, outward mobility will be reemphasized under the new internationalization strategy (please refer to the Higher Education Authority for further details).

Education Ireland has worked jointly with DAAD, the British Council, and CampusFrance to promote European education in Thailand and Mexico.

International Students in Ireland

At present there are approximately 26,000 international students in higher education in Ireland, about one-third of who come from European countries. These figures include exchange and Junior Year Abroad (JYA) students.

The United States is the single most important country of origin for international students in HEIs in Ireland, with over 6,000 U.S. students choosing to study abroad in Ireland during the 2008/09 academic year. Figures from the *2009 Open Doors Report*, compiled by the Institute of International Education (IIE), indicated a 19 percent increase in the number of study abroad students from the U.S. studying in Ireland in the 2007/08 academic year[1] and also reported that after China, Ireland was the fastest growing destination for U.S. study abroad students.

Traditional associations and major academic and business partnerships make North America an obvious focal point for Irish HEIs. Education Ireland, in conjunction with other institutions, is involved in a number of strategic campaigns in the U.S., highlighting the quality and value of Irish education.

After the U.S., China is the next most important country of origin for international students in Ireland, followed by France, the UK, Germany, Spain, and Malaysia.

Brief Profile of International Students in Ireland:[2]

- The income from international students in higher education (not including airfares and family visits, etc.) is around €500 million per year.

- Over two-thirds of international students are taking full-time programs (an increase of ten percent since 2006/07).

- There are now over 2,000 international students taking Ph.D. programs in Ireland—a dramatic increase over the last three years, and a reflection of the national emphasis on higher level research. At eight percent of the total international student cohort, Ireland's Ph.D. enrollments are well above international averages. The numbers taking Master's programs have also increased. Postgraduate study is particularly focused on science-related disciplines, but there is evidence of growth across every discipline.

- EU exchange numbers have decreased from 2006/07, but full-time EU and European student numbers have increased.

- Female students dominate slightly, accounting for 54 percent of the cohort, but there are significant differences by place of origin.

- In comparison to 2006/07, international student numbers have decreased from China, the UK, Spain, Italy, Singapore, Japan and South Korea (in most cases as a result of a decline in language students).

- International students have increased from most other countries, notably, France, Canada, Nigeria, Saudi Arabia, Brazil and Romania, and regionally from Central and Eastern Europe and Latin America and the Caribbean.

- JYA/Study Abroad students have increased by over 20 percent.

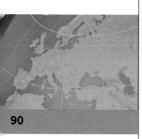

■ Humanities, creative arts, and business-related subjects are the most important academic disciplines for international students in Ireland.

■ International student enrollments in the field of medicine have declined in line with government policy to increase the availability of places to Irish students. However, in comparison to other countries, the number of international students taking courses in medicine in Ireland is high.

Education Ireland: Education Ireland promotes Ireland as a destination for a high quality education and provides comprehensive information on studying in Ireland for prospective students through its website, social media sites and electronic and printed materials. Education Ireland is managed by Enterprise Ireland (EI), the Irish government agency responsible for the development and promotion of the business sector.

---

[1] IIE data includes figures on study abroad students on programs managed by their home institutions, which are not captured under the Irish study, as these students are not formally registered in Irish HEIs. Source: *Open Doors 2009: Report on International Educational Exchange.* New York: Institute of International Education.

[2] Education Ireland, "International Students in Higher Education in Ireland, 2009/2010," May 2010. http://www.educationireland.ie/index.php?option=com_rokdownloads&view=file&Itemid=100355&id=29:international-students-in-higher-education-in-ireland-2010-final.

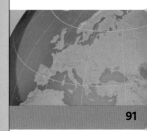

REGION: **Europe**

COUNTRY: **Netherlands**

By Netherlands Organization for International Cooperation in Higher Education (Nuffic)

In a 2008 Internationalization Agenda, the Ministry of Education addressed the importance of promoting international student mobility in the Netherlands, noting the value international students provide toward improving overall quality and performance in Dutch higher education and benefiting those students who stay at home.

Due to current demographic shifts, institutions in Europe are increasingly faced with the challenge of sustaining enrollments in the future. This has, in turn, created competition within Europe for high quality students. The Dutch knowledge economy depends on its institutions being able to attract students from within and outside Europe and prepare highly skilled graduates for the labor market, who can positively contribute to the skills, knowledge and creativity pool of the Netherlands. Those students returning to their home country or moving to other destinations function as ambassadors of Dutch higher education and have the potential to create or sustain economic, political and cultural ties with the Netherlands. For the same reason, a key priority is sending more Dutch students abroad, who return and benefit from having international and intercultural competencies.

Netherlands Organization for International Cooperation in Higher Education (Nuffic) is responsible for the promotion and marketing of Dutch higher education abroad. Its "Study in Holland" activities aim to attract students to the Netherlands. Nuffic also supports Dutch students who wish to study abroad through the "WilWeg" activities, by providing them information on practical, financial or legal issues. Furthermore, Nuffic has

REGION:
Europe
COUNTRY:
Netherlands

established the Holland Alumni Network for foreign students that have studied in the Netherlands: www.hollandalumni.nl.

Nuffic focuses on the education promotion and marketing in specific countries through a network of ten Netherlands Education Support Offices ("NESO"), located in China, India, Indonesia, Brazil, Vietnam, Thailand, Mexico, Russia, Taiwan and South Korea. These offices promote Study-in-Holland, collect and disseminate information on higher education in these countries, advise local students on learning opportunities in the Netherlands and support Dutch institutions in their activities and cooperation in these countries. Furthermore Holland alumni networks in these countries are supported by Nuffic NESO's.

facts and figures

- There were over 55,000 international students in Dutch higher education in 2009.

- The top five places of origin in 2009 were Germany, China, Belgium, Spain and France.

- Nuffic is an independent, non-profit organization that supports internationalization in higher education and research in the Netherlands.

Source: Nuffic

Many important steps have been taken over the past two decades to facilitate student mobility. International students who would like to take paid work alongside their studies are allowed to do so. Depending on nationality, students can only do this for a limited amount of hours per week and only if the employer has applied for a work permit. Immigration has become more flexible for international students and so-called "knowledge workers" with the adoption of new immigration policy and regulations in 2010. However some obstacles still persist, especially for students from most non-EU countries. Dutch researchers who go abroad on a scholarship are not always entitled to social security and pension rights. These benefits depend on having tenure, which grant holders often do not have. In the past decade, national security regulations have made it more difficult for students from certain countries (for instance Iran and North Korea) to study in the Netherlands. This is especially the case for programs related to nuclear technology.

To support and promote student mobility, Nuffic administers a range of international scholarship programs targeted to both outbound and inbound students. The organization also raises awareness of the importance of international cooperation with policy makers and other relevant stakeholders. Through consultations with national and international data providers, Nuffic tries to continuously search for better ways to reflect the current reality in international mobility and through research on various types of mobility. Nuffic's annual *Internationalization Monitor* includes updated quantitative information on student and academic mobility, which has come to serve as an important publication to monitor mobility developments of various governments and institutions.

Nuffic also implements programs specifically aimed at strengthening the performance of individuals, organizations and institutions in developing countries or to help them develop their capacities by extending their expertise, know-how and skills. The lack of advanced capacity is generally considered as an important restriction for socio-economic development. The Netherlands Ministry of Foreign Affairs therefore finances a number of international education programs for a number of developing countries with capacity development as the main objective. Nuffic manages these programs. For example, the Netherlands Initiative for Capacity Development in Higher Education (NICHE) program aims to strengthen institutional capacity in 23 developing countries for institutions and organizations providing post-secondary education and training.

At the individual level, Nuffic administers scholarship programs for the benefit of international students (e.g. Huygens Scholarship Program or Netherlands Fellowships Program) and collects and disseminates information on studying abroad or studying in the Netherlands. Key services to the institutions include the recognition of degrees and prior qualifications of students applying to these institutions, support in student recruitment, brokerage in institutional cooperation in the NESO countries, and the selection and management of capacity-building processes. On these topics, Nuffic has also developed expertise and shares this expertise

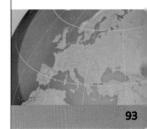

93

REGION:
Europe
COUNTRY:
Netherlands

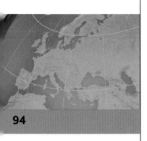

94

through research, consultancy and courses. On a broad national level, Nuffic functions as a center of expertise on international cooperation in higher education and is responsible for the promotion and branding of Dutch higher education.

On a regional European level, Nuffic works with partner organizations and members of the Academic Cooperation Association (ACA), an independent European organization dedicated to the management, analysis and improvement of education and training cooperation within Europe and between Europe and other parts of the world. In addition, there are various project partnerships with these and other international partners to promote regional mobility. Multilateral regional cooperation takes place through the intergovernmental Bologna Process. Important objectives have been to make European higher education more attractive for international students and to foster student and staff mobility within the European Higher Education Area. The first objective has clearly been achieved. Internal mobility however is still increasing slower than projected.

Nuffic is in many ways involved in facilitating further mobility in higher education. Nuffic is at the forefront of the international discussion on recognition. The organization has been designated by the Netherlands Ministry of Education, Culture and Science as the Dutch recognition information center for two European networks: the National Academic Recognition Information Centre (NARIC) and the European National Information Centre on Recognition and Mobility (ENIC). In this field, Nuffic works for all organizations that encounter foreign diplomas in the course of their business, such as universities, other higher education institutions, companies and ministries.

Nuffic offers services and products in the field of credential evaluation, and foreign diploma and course equivalencies evaluation for both inbound and outbound students in addition to determining recognition qualifications of non-Dutch programs and institutions. Dutch diplomas are evaluated by preparing "diploma descriptions" for individuals who have been awarded a higher education diploma in the Netherlands, and who wish to work or study abroad. These descriptions provide information about academic qualifications obtained in the Netherlands, and also offer suggestions on how the qualification should be evaluated in the country in which it is presented.

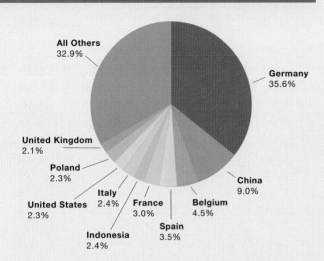

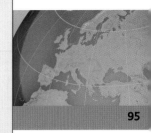

95

Figure 12: Places of Origin of International Students in the Netherlands, 2009

Source: Nuffic

Nuffic also supports institutions in their internationalization efforts. It does so by providing consultancy services to universities and by issuing publications on internationalization and international cooperation. As of 2009, Nuffic has offered a self-evaluation and benchmarking tool for higher education institutions, the MINT tool (Mapping INTernationalization) which is currently available for use. With the help of this tool, universities (or faculties and/or schools) or programs can map their internationalization efforts and compare their efforts with other universities or programs.

Both the Dutch Ministry of Education and Nuffic are committed to increasing the international character of Dutch universities and the Dutch student population. Mobility plays a central role in this strategy. With the ongoing globalization of labor markets and the export-oriented economy of the Netherlands, an international outlook is seen as one of the necessary competences for Dutch graduates. The increasing integration of the European higher education area has widened the European playing field for many Dutch universities, as mobility to and from these European partner countries

is becoming more common. Yet, there are still many obstacles in the way, be it in the form of recognition issues, financial barriers or other obstacles. Nuffic contributes in removing these obstacles where possible or mitigating their impact in other cases.

Nuffic (Netherlands Organization for International Cooperation in Higher Education): As an independent, non-profit organization based in The Hague, the Netherlands, Nuffic supports internationalization in higher education and research in the Netherlands and abroad, and helps improve access to higher education worldwide.

REGION: **Europe**

COUNTRY: **Spain**

By Fundación Universidad.es

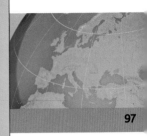

In October 2008, the Spanish federal government, alongside regional governments and Spanish universities, approved the creation of a foundation for the international promotion of Spanish universities—Universidad.es. The main purpose of the organization is to create an international brand for the Spanish university system and to improve the international visibility of Spanish universities, both public and private. One of the main lines of action developed by this agency is to promote student mobility in Spain, establishing the country as a leading destination for international students and researchers and increasing the presence of Spanish students and researchers throughout the world.

At a national level, public diplomacy and enhanced training of Spanish students and researchers are the main drivers for outbound mobility. The country aims to attract international students in line with the growing priority placed on internationalization among Spanish institutions, which includes creating an international and multicultural environment on university campuses, and contributing to capacity building in developing countries through the establishment of mobility programs.

In order to fulfill its main objectives to support Spain's student mobility objectives, Universidad.es Foundation works closely with the governmental and higher education sectors. At the federal level, the organization has a close working relationship with the Ministry of Education and with all other governmental departments in charge of higher education both at national and regional levels. The relationship with the Ministry of Foreign Affairs and

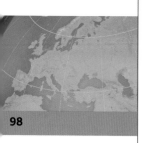

Cooperation and with the Spanish Agency for International Development and Cooperation is particularly important for the development of projects and programs with developing countries.

Taking into account some of the hindrances to mobility and exchange—namely the process of obtaining a visa to study or conduct research in Spain—the Foundation is organizing a working group composed of stakeholders in the institutional and government arenas to respond to easing the visa process. The main purpose of this initiative will be to analyze the main challenges and propose policy recommendations and alternatives for simplifying the process of obtaining student visas.

In the higher education sector, both public and private higher education institutions are represented by Universidad.es Foundation. All of the organization's activities are developed in close cooperation with universities both individually and through the Conference of Rectors of the Spanish Universities.

Universidad.es also aims to establish individual strategies in order to attract students and researchers from countries of strategic importance in the international higher education market for Spain, including Argentina, Brazil, Chile, China, Colombia, Equatorial Guinea, India, Italy, Morocco, Mexico, Portugal, Russia, Syria, Saudi Arabia, and the United States.

Universidad.es Foundation has developed a website mainly oriented to an international audience. International students and researchers can find in www.universidad.es a useful tool that may help them organize an academic stay in Spain. This dedicated website features comprehensive information on Spanish universities and their academic programs, a complete and updated scholarships database, and information on formal and legal requirements for organizing an academic stay within Spain. Additionally, an online student and researcher service has been recently launched through the Foundation's website. This service allows users to contact Universidad.es through three channels: by phone, by sending their questions by e-mail, or live through the new chat system.

Since its creation in 2009, Universidad.es Foundation has worked closely with sister organizations from different countries. Along with national agencies from other European countries, Universidad.es has organized a series of higher education fairs focused on post-graduate courses in different countries

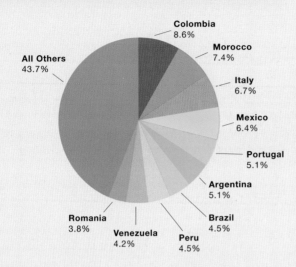

Figure 13: Places of Origin of International Students in Spain, 2008/09

Source: Ministry of Education of Spain
Note: The data in the figure refers to "foreign students" only and not to "mobile students."

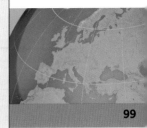

REGION:
Europe
COUNTRY:
Spain

in Latin America. The organization has also participated in a similar initiative carried out by European national agencies with the support of the European Commission in Asia.

This regional approach of promoting student mobility in Europe has been well received by partner institutions and other stakeholders. Collaborative events and fairs have been useful not only for promoting each country's higher education system abroad, but also for contributing to the development and internationalization of higher education both in Europe and in the partner regions.

While Universidad.es Foundation does not currently collect primary data on student mobility, the organization works with the Ministry of Education's statistics service in order to improve the quality of the international higher education data they collect in an effort to conform to international standards. A project for the collection of data on the mobility of students, researchers, lecturers and university staff, gathered directly from Spanish

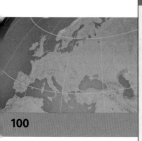

REGION:
Europe
COUNTRY:
Spain

facts and figures

- There were over 65,000 international students in Spain in 2008/09.

- The top five places of origin in 2008/09 were Colombia, Morocco, Italy, Mexico and Portugal.

- Nearly 24,000 Spanish students studied abroad in other countries in 2008/09.

- Universidad.es, a new Foundation representing all Spanish universities, will focus on policy recommendations to facilitate increased student mobility and exchange.

Source: Fundación Universidad.es

universities, has been recently launched and the first results of this project are expected during the first semester of 2011. The information that Universidad.es Foundation currently has regarding student mobility in Spain shows that further efforts must be made to increase its status as an attractive destination for international students. This data has been used to bolster the support of governmental initiatives focused on fostering academic mobility in Spain, which should aid in this objective moving forward.

The Foundation for the International Promotion of Spanish Universities: Universidad.es is an initiative of the Spanish government together with Spain's regional governments and the universities themselves. Its main aim is to create an international brand of the Spanish University, maximizing its international visibility and providing effective reputation management.

REGION: **Europe**

COUNTRY: **Sweden**

By the Swedish Institute

Successive Swedish governments have long regarded the internationalization of higher education as something positive for Swedish higher education. It remains one of several means to internationalize the study experience for Swedish students who do not go abroad, and a way to improve the quality of Swedish higher education. International students have been funded in the same way that national students have been funded (i.e., through government funding to higher education institutions) and there have only been rare cases where international students have been required to pay any kind of tuition fees. Development aid has also been an important motive, although there has been some concern in recent years that too much focus on inbound mobility could lead to brain drain in relation to some lower income countries.

A sharp increase in the number of English-taught courses and a consequential increase in the number of inbound students in the last decade, coupled with the rise of a global education market, has led to a gradual change in policy from the government. As of 2011, students from countries outside the European Union (EU) will be charged the full cost of studies in Sweden. The government has two principal motives for introducing tuition fees for students from outside the EU: 1) The mounting costs for international students, and 2) Sweden should attract foreign students because of the quality of its higher education, not because of free tuition. However, the government also plans to appropriate at least 90 million SEK (approximately USD 12 million) for scholarships, partly aimed at students from lower income countries.

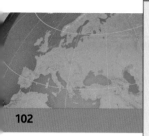

102

REGION:
Europe
COUNTRY:
Sweden

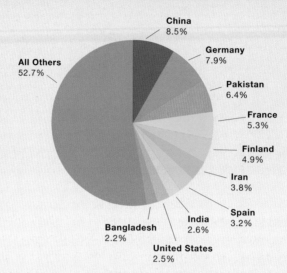

China
8.5%

Germany
7.9%

All Others
52.7%

Pakistan
6.4%

France
5.3%

Finland
4.9%

Iran
3.8%

Spain
3.2%

India
2.6%

Bangladesh
2.2%

United States
2.5%

Figure 14: Places of Origin of International Students in Sweden, 2008/09

Source: Swedish Institute

Public diplomacy has historically not been a very prominent motive for inbound student mobility, although there are signs that it might be given more weight in the future. Other motives that are likely to gain more weight are skills shortages and the connection between attracting foreign students and attracting foreign investments.

The Swedish Institute, a government agency for public and cultural diplomacy, has supported international mobility in higher education since the 1940s through the provision of scholarships for inbound and outbound students. Many of the scholarships were provided through bilateral agreements with other countries. Since the 1970s there have been development aid-funded scholarships for Master's and Ph.D. studies in Sweden. Since the late 1990s, the government has funded extensive scholarship programs aimed at exchange with countries in Eastern Europe and the former Soviet Union.

Since 1989, Swedish students have been able to obtain loans to study abroad. Sweden participates in the various EU-sponsored mobility schemes, most notably ERASMUS and Erasmus Mundus, in higher education. Sweden joined in 1992, and since the early 1990s, the number of outbound students increased sharply to reach around 30,000 per year.

Meanwhile, in the 1990s the number of English-taught programs at the Master's level started to increase, as did the number of international students. This led eventually to a balance being achieved between the number of inbound and the number of outbound students in the early 2000s. In the last few years, the number of inbound students has exceeded that of outbound students, which has led to new measures by the government to stimulate outbound mobility, by providing funding for teacher mobility and encouraging the study of more foreign languages in secondary school.

Mobility programs are managed and funded through several government offices and private organizations. The International Program Office (IPK) handles the administration of EU programs (including ERASMUS and Erasmus Mundus) and several aid-funded programs that also promote mobility. STINT, The Foundation for the Internationalization of Research, has also provided funding for inbound mobility. The Swedish Institute cooperates with IPK, STINT and the Swedish National Agency for Higher Education (HSV) to promote and advocate for student mobility. Additionally, the Swedish Institute also works with higher education institutions within Sweden to support student mobility. In 2008, the Swedish Institute and 29 higher education institutions jointly launched a collaborative project to promote Sweden as a study destination.

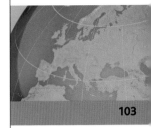

103

REGION:
Europe
COUNTRY:
Sweden

facts and figures

■ There were over 36,000 international students in Sweden in 2008/09.

■ The top five places of origin in 2008/09 were China, Germany, Pakistan, France and Finland.

■ More than 24,000 Swedish students studied abroad in other countries in 2008/09.

(Source: Swedish Institute)

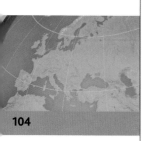

The Swedish Institute administers ten scholarship programs directed to international students and researchers from different regions and countries. Approximately 1,000 international students receive these funding awards for short- and long-term programs. International students in Ph.D. programs and researchers receive scholarships for six or 12 months; Master's students can receive funding for up to two years. Despite these general guidelines, funding duration can vary by program. For example, a scholarship program financed by the Pakistan Higher Education Commission and administered by the Swedish Institute enables Pakistani students to spend up to six years in Sweden for a Master's degree program followed by a doctoral degree.

In line with regional mobility efforts, the Swedish Institute Baltic Sea Region Exchange program supports cooperation in education and research between Sweden and Belarus, Estonia, Latvia, Lithuania, Poland, Russia and Ukraine. Funding is available for projects or networking activities as well as for individual scholarships and grants for short-term visits. The program targets students, teachers, researchers, administrators and doctoral students in high school education, adult education, undergraduate studies and advanced research.

As a member organization of Academic Cooperation Association (ACA), the Swedish Institute, along with the IPK, cooperates with other member organizations on issues that relate to international mobility. While the Swedish Institute does not collect mobility data—the HSV and Statistics Sweden are the agencies primarily responsible for data collection and reporting at the national level—the Institute engages in research on international student experiences and perceptions, used to promote Sweden as a study destination. These analyses and data have been used to advocate for policies that will attract more international students to Sweden in the years ahead.

Swedish Institute: The Swedish Institute (SI) is a public agency that promotes interest and confidence in Sweden around the world. SI seeks to establish cooperation and lasting relations with other countries through strategic communication and exchange in the fields of culture, education, science and business. SI also supports Swedish language instruction at foreign universities.

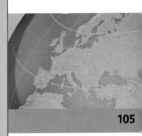

International student mobility offers the opportunity to build more connections between individuals across countries through educational and cultural exchange, equipping a new generation with the skills and understanding they will need to rise to global challenges, now and in the future. The British Council views the exchange of students among nations as one of the most effective public diplomacy tools. Students who spend time immersed in another culture graduate more open-minded, well-rounded, and accustomed to varying perspectives. Study abroad equips United Kingdom (UK) students with the vital skills they need to prosper in a global economy as they enter the workforce of their home country and develop in their careers. It also sets the stage for greater collaboration and exchange of ideas among the world's best and brightest young minds.

Inward Mobility

International students contribute immeasurably to the intellectual vitality of UK education, making a critical contribution to the UK's research capacity and its standing in the globalized knowledge economy. The presence of international students on campus also helps to ensure that a greater diversity of programs is available for UK students; they provide a driver to maintain high quality course provision as UK universities compete in an increasingly competitive market to attract them; they enrich the diversity of campuses and communities and help to broaden the outlook and understanding of UK students as they prepare to join a global workplace.

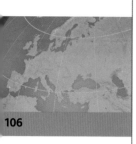

REGION:
Europe
COUNTRY:
United Kingdom

The British Council has been working to ensure that students, agents and educational communities around the world understand the new system and the benefits it offers. The organization provides information, guidance and support, whether face-to-face via pre-departure briefings or walk-in centers, on the Education UK website, and through publications, marketing and PR campaigns. As well as these in-country communications and guidance activities, the British Council also works closely with the UK Border Agency (UKBA) to share observations and help to ensure any problems are addressed.

Outward Mobility

The motivations for outward mobility include the academic and personal development of the student, language development of the student, and the wider cultural relation implications for the UK. An important mechanism to support student mobility within Europe is ERASMUS. This program enables higher education students, teachers and institutions in 31 European countries to study for part of their degree in another country. ERASMUS covers all European Union (EU) countries plus Norway, Lichtenstein, Iceland and Turkey. It is relevant to both inbound and outbound students from the UK. The British Council is the agency responsible for managing funding relating to outwardly mobile students. Through administering ERASMUS in the UK, the British Council organizes events to assist and inform UK institutions, and produces literature and posters to assist UK institutions to promote ERASMUS among domestic students.

The 'fee waiver' is a government-led initiative introduced in 1999 which ensures that UK students who are studying outside of the UK for a year do not have to pay fees to their home institution (and students mobile under ERASMUS would have their host institution fees covered). In effect, these students receive a fee-free year of study, which can prove quite an incentive to outward mobility. Approximately 5,525 UK students were eligible to receive this waiver in 2008/09.[1]

National Mobility Initiatives of the UK

The Prime Minister's Initiative for International Education (PMI2) is a five-year strategy, launched in 2006, which aims to support UK engagement in the global education arena. It does so by promoting UK higher education and by providing a mechanism for education institutions in the UK to link strategically with counterparts overseas. The elements of the PMI2 are:

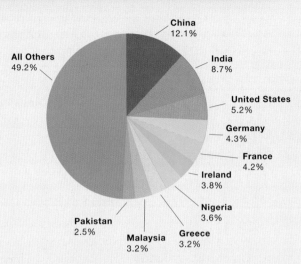

Figure 15: Places of Origin of International Students in the UK, 2008/09

Source: HESA data provided by British Council

REGION:
Europe
COUNTRY:
United Kingdom

■ Higher and Further (Vocational) Education Partnerships aimed at building the UK's profile as a valued partner in education.

■ Marketing and communications - Providing a national brand and communications platform for UK education as both partner and educator, and providing information to help students access UK education opportunities.

■ Enhancing the quality of the international student experience in the UK through benchmarking and sharing best practices.

■ Enhancing the employability of international graduate students.

Other Initiatives Managed by the British Council

■ *International Strategic Partnerships in Research and Education (INSPIRE)* is a British Council funded project that aims to significantly strengthen academic and research partnerships between Higher Education Institutions (HEIs) in the UK and in Afghanistan, Bangladesh, Kazakhstan, Pakistan and Uzbekistan. The principal aim of INSPIRE

108

- There were over 415,000 international students in public post-secondary institutions the UK in 2008/09.

- The top five places of origin in 2008/09 were China, India, U.S., Germany and France.

- According to UNESCO, nearly 22,000 students from the UK studied abroad in other countries in 2007/08, and over 10,000 additional students from UK took part in ERASMUS in 2007/08.

- The Prime Minister's Initiative for International Education (PMI2) is a five-year national strategy, launched in 2006, which aims to support UK engagement in the global education arena.

Sources: British Council, UNESCO, ERASMUS

is to support a significant increase in the number and scope of higher education partnerships between the UK and universities in the Central and South Asia Region.

- *Development Partnerships in Higher Education (DelPHE)* provides funding for higher education institutions working collaboratively on development goals. In addition to addressing core areas such as health, basic education and gender equality, DelPHE's aim is to encourage projects that promote science and technology in Africa and Asia. DelPHE is funded by the Department for International Development.

- *UK–India Education and Research Initiative (UKIERI)* is a five-year program which aims to substantially improve educational links between India and the UK. The program has been recognized as playing an important role in fostering contacts across the UK and India in the field of higher education.

- *Education Partnerships in Africa (EPA)* is a program for English higher education and further education institutions wishing to work in partnership with counterparts in sub-Saharan Africa. EPA is supporting 72 partnerships between English further education and higher education institutions and sub-Saharan African universities and education and training institutions. The partnerships build institutional capacity to deliver employability skills in collaboration with local employers and social enterprises.

Further Work of the British Council

For some of these major initiatives and programs, the British Council is contracted by the UK government to manage and promote inward and outward student mobility. The British Council manages several additional scholarship programs including Chevening (funded by the UK Foreign and Commonwealth office), the UK 9/11 Scholarships Fund and others.

The British Council has also collaborated with other EU organizations including Nuffic (Netherlands), CampusFrance, and DAAD (Germany) to organize a series of education fairs in Malaysia, Philippines and other countries.

British Council: Connecting the UK to the world and the world to the UK, the British Council is Britain's international cultural relations body.

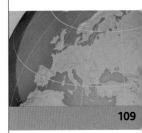

109

REGION:
Europe
COUNTRY:
United Kingdom

---

[1]   Source: British Council analysis of ERASMUS and Higher Education Statistics Agency (HESA) data.

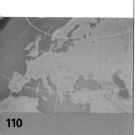

110

REGION: **Oceania**

Australia and New Zealand, the two largest countries in the region, attract many students from Asian countries such as China, India and Malaysia. Mobile students from Australia and New Zealand largely study in Oceania, in the U.S. or in the United Kingdom.

In both Australia and New Zealand, the enrollment of international students as a percentage of total higher education enrollments is the highest in the world. In New Zealand, over 28 percent of all university students are international and over 23 percent in Australia. These percentages are even higher for graduate students. For example, 32 percent of doctoral students in New Zealand are international students.

These countries also support the outbound mobility of their students through various scholarship opportunities and funding grants. According to research conducted by the Australian Universities International Directors' Forum (AUIDF), in 2009/10 a total of 32 percent of Australian students undertaking international study experiences went to Asia, compared to 37 percent who went to Europe, and 22 percent who took up studies in the Americas.

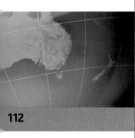

The major players in international education in Oceania are looking to attract more students, with a particular emphasis on drawing doctoral candidates and researchers from abroad. The biggest challenge in meeting these goals is providing adequate funding to attract the best candidates. Australia and New Zealand are competing with other world regions to identify public and private funding sources as well as to adapt education policies to attract well-qualified international students. At the same time, governments are tightening visa policies to ensure that the institutions that host international students are qualified to receive them and are properly screening their incoming students before admission. Universities are also looking to expand branch campuses around the world, and to expand their "off-shore" delivery of courses and degrees.

The other nations of Oceania, including Fiji and the Marshall Islands, have relatively small numbers of inbound and outgoing mobile students, but have also seen mobility numbers increasing steadily.

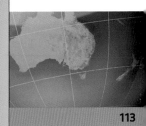

REGION: **Oceania**

COUNTRY: **Australia**

By Australian Education International (AEI)

International education and mobility has been actively promoted and supported by the Australian Government for decades. To support the flow of international students to and from the country, opportunities have been created by the Australian Government through sponsored exchange programs and scholarships. These are intended to foster long-lasting education, research and professional linkages between individuals, institutions and countries. These links help to further strengthen the bilateral ties between Australia and countries throughout the world.

Australia's inbound student mobility goals were elaborated by former Minister for Education, Julia Gillard, in her address to the 2009 Australian International Education Conference, and include:

■ Ensuring that Australia is seen as a welcoming and valuable place to study for a globally recognized qualification.

■ Enhancing international awareness of Australia as a leader in education, research and learning.

■ Showcasing Australia's innovativeness, quality and global reputation for world-class education, training and research.

■ Ensuring that Australia's education and training industry is provided with the support and assistance it needs for sustainable growth.

In 2010, Senator Chris Evans, the Minister for Tertiary Education, stated that, "a high quality international education sector benefits all. It produces better-educated, more worldly students from Australia and overseas; it

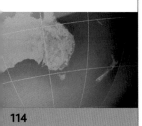

REGION:
Oceania
COUNTRY:
Australia

encourages new intellectual perspectives, higher academic standards and new research links. It enriches our nation."

Australia's international education sector has experienced considerable growth in recent years. Between 2002 and 2009, international student enrollments across all education sectors (including universities, English language colleges, vocational education colleges and high schools) grew by an average annual rate of 13 percent—more than doubling over this time. In 2009, nearly half a million students studied in Australia on a student visa. The majority of international students studying in Australia pay full tuition fees. However, the Australian Government provides scholarship assistance totalling around A$200 million per year to many international students, in addition to other scholarships offered by Australian universities.

The Australian Government is equally committed to supporting Australian students to engage in study abroad experiences in other countries. Outbound mobility is seen as a mechanism to improve the quality of education that Australian graduates receive so that Australian business remains internationally competitive into the future. Outbound mobility contributes to both of these goals by providing students with intercultural competence as well as unique skills and knowledge that only come when an individual is immersed in another society.

Outbound mobility gives Australian students the opportunity to become global citizens, exposing them to different and unfamiliar situations, different approaches to problem solving and different ways of relating to each other. The Australian Government supports outbound mobility because as the cohort of Australian graduates with an international study experience grows, so too does Australia's global competitiveness. The nation's ability to be a leading knowledge economy—to have the skilled people that are needed to compete globally and to deal with the challenges of the future in key areas such as security and climate change—will depend on how well Australians can communicate and collaborate on the world stage.

In recognition of the importance of outbound mobility to Australia's interests, the Australian Government has initiated and sponsored a wide range of activities over the past few years to assist the sector in facilitating greater student mobility by Australians, including:

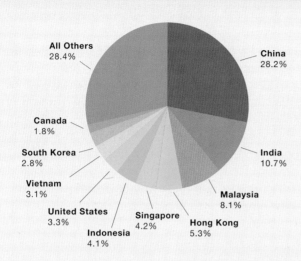

Figure 16: Places of Origin of International Students in Australia, 2009

Source: AEI

REGION:
Oceania
COUNTRY:
Australia

■ *The Study Overseas Short Term Mobility Program*—provides funding to Australian universities to support their students to undertake group based short-term international mobility experiences such as: short-term study tours and research trips of between three weeks and six months in duration, internships and work placements, practicum and clinical placements.

■ *The Prime Minister's Australia Asia Awards*—annually support 60 of the best and brightest university students from Australia and Asia to undertake an international research, study and internship experience to build a network of people across the region that have a strong affinity with Australia and develop an internationally-aware, skilled workforce in Australia.

■ *The Vocational Education & Training (VET) Outbound Mobility Program*—the program provides funding for VET students and staff to undertake an international study opportunity or work placement in a variety of countries within the Asia-Pacific region, the Middle East, Europe and the Americas. The program aims to increase the number of

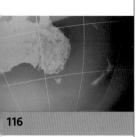

Australian vocational education and training ("VET") students undertaking an international study experience and increase the level of partnerships between Australian and international VET training providers and industry.

■ *The European Union (EU)/Australia Cooperation in Higher Education and VET Projects*—is a consortia of student mobility projects for Australian students in higher education and VET, aiming to develop joint credit transfer arrangements, support academic cooperation and encourage student mobility within Australia and the EU.

The Australian Government, through Australian Education International (AEI) in the Department of Education, Employment and Workplace Relations, has established policies that support these overall goals of encouraging and increasing inbound and outbound student mobility, in the following key areas:

■ *Funding of research and other projects* for student mobility that provides more accurate statistical data, a snapshot of the demographic make-up and nature of student mobility in Australia, and an overview of current student mobility practices at Australian universities.

■ *Funding of exchange scholarships* to universities and vocational education training organizations that assist them to provide incoming and outgoing student mobility scholarships and support the establishment of long-term exchange partners that promote mobility.

■ *Funding of Endeavor Awards* at post-graduate, vocational education and training ("VET") and professional levels for Australian and international scholars and professionals to undertake research and build collaborations.

■ *Promotion* of outbound mobility through the establishment of an overseas study portal which consolidates information about overseas study opportunities for Australian students into one easy-to-access site.

The Australian Government works with the higher education sector to promote and support student mobility through individual student scholarships that are provided to and distributed by institutions for promoting student mobility. The government also provides funding to institutions to establish and build linkages with international partners and coordinates promotional efforts at a national level through its Overseas Study Portal (www.studyoverseas.gov.au) that profiles all Australian universities and their

- There were over 245,000 international students in Australian higher education in 2009.

- The top five places of origin were China, India, Malaysia, Hong Kong and Singapore.

- Australian Education International (AEI) in the Department of Education, Employment and Workplace Relations sets policies and funds research, scholarships, and an online study portal.

Source: AEI

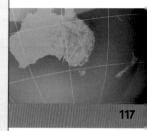

117

REGION:
Oceania
COUNTRY:
Australia

student mobility programs. This is also promoted with high school career advisers as students consider their tertiary study options.

While a large number of Australian students still undertake study at more "traditional" destinations such as the United Kingdom, the United States and Canada, students from Australia are increasingly exploring opportunities in countries such as China, India, Indonesia, Japan, South Korea and Vietnam. The aim of government initiatives such as the National Asian Languages Studies in Schools Program (NALSSP) and the Prime Minister's Australia Asia Awards are to ensure that Australia is the most Asian-literate western country in the world.

Australia was one of the inaugural countries involved in the establishment of the University Mobility in Asia and the Pacific (UMAP) Program in 1993. This program assisted in support of partnerships, credit transfer and institutional relationships that fostered student mobility in the Asia Pacific Region. Currently, the Australian UMAP Student Exchange Program provides funding to Australian higher education institutions to subsidize the cost of establishing and monitoring Australian students' participation in UMAP student exchanges with counterpart higher education institutions in the region. The benefits of this association have been a regional commitment to reducing barriers to educational exchange by working through issues such as credit transfer, as well as promoting the opportunity and value of mobility with institutions and students.

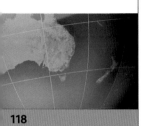

REGION:
Oceania
COUNTRY:
Australia

In addition to the UMAP Student Exchange Program, the Australian Government also administers the Endeavour Student Exchange program and the Endeavour Cheung Kong Student Exchange Program. These programs provide funding to Australian higher education institutions to enable undergraduate Bachelor degree students in all disciplines to undertake at least one semester and no more than two semesters of study at an accredited higher education institution in an eligible country. Student exchanges that are eligible under the three exchange programs include provisions for tuition fee waivers and credit transfer. Australian higher education institutions receive A$5,000 per student (excluding Goods and Services Tax) to subsidize the cost of the student's participation in an eligible student exchange.

Australian Education International: As the international arm of the Australian Government's Department of Education, Employment and Workplace Relations (DEEWR), Australian Education International (AEI) provides leadership across all levels of government and industry to support the sustainable development of a world-class and globally connected international education and training system in Australia.

REGION: **Oceania**

COUNTRY: **New Zealand**

By the New Zealand Ministry of Education

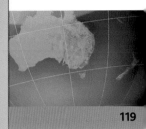

The New Zealand government encourages the enrollment of international students through public and private education providers. This activity is viewed as beneficial in increasing recognition of New Zealand qualifications, expanding international awareness by New Zealand students, and in providing fee revenues for providers. In addition to supporting the recruitment of fee-paying students, whose combined economic impact totaled NZ$2.1 billion during the 2007/08 financial year, the government also provides a number of scholarships as part of an overseas aid program.

The New Zealand government has implemented a range of policies to support international student mobility. This began with the Education Act 1989, legislation that explicitly authorized the recruitment of international fee-paying students by public education providers (including schools, universities, and technical institutes). Following marked growth in international student enrollments, a compulsory "Code of Practice for the Pastoral Care of International Students" was initially implemented by the Ministry of Education in 2002, and amended in 2003 and 2010. The Code of Practice is required to be followed by any education provider that enrolls international students.

Since 2004, the government has funded the international promotion of New Zealand education as a national brand, and has offered scholarships for top doctoral and undergraduate students. These and other programs are administered by the lead sector body for international education, the Education New Zealand Trust. The funding of national promotions efforts

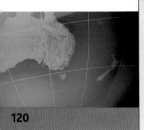

120

REGION:
Oceania
COUNTRY:
New Zealand

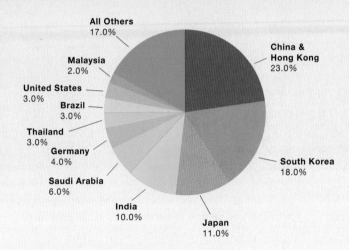

Figure 17: Places of Origin of International Students in New Zealand, 2009

Source: New Zealand Ministry of Education

Note: These data include "fee-paying" students for calendar year 2009.

is also supported through the compulsory Export Education Levy, which has been charged to education providers since 2003. The rate of the Export Education Levy is 0.45 percent of tuition revenues from international students. In 2009, the promotions efforts targeted among specific countries have led to a general increase in interest in New Zealand education options.

A successful policy to attract more research students to New Zealand universities allows for international students pursuing Ph.D. programs to pay domestic student fee rates instead of higher international student rates. This policy was implemented in 2006, and has resulted in a very marked rise in enrollments of this group of international students. Total enrollments of international Ph.D. students at New Zealand's eight universities rose from 693 during the 2005 calendar year to 2,405 during the 2009 calendar year.

Over 7,000 New Zealand students study abroad in other countries each year. Of these students, approximately 74 percent study at Australian higher education institutions, 13 percent go to U.S. colleges and universities, and eight percent study in the UK. Small numbers enroll in institutions in Japan and Germany, and in South East Asian nations.

Governance and Advocacy

Various Departments and Ministries are involved in international student affairs related to mobility and exchange. The Department of Labour is primarily responsible for immigration issues and overseeing the administration of the Immigration Act, while the Ministry of Education provides advice to this Department on proposals to modify student visa regulations. Sector bodies and education providers, which have an interest in recruiting international students, are known to advocate publicly and privately for changes to existing student visa regulations.

The Ministry of Education is the government's lead advisor on the New Zealand education system, shaping direction for sector agencies and providers.

The Ministry undertakes wide consultation with sector bodies and education providers in developing strategies and policies for student mobility. These sector bodies and providers include groups representing universities, the institutes of technology and polytechnics, schools, and private providers.

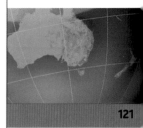

121

REGION:
Oceania
COUNTRY:
New Zealand

facts and figures

- There were over 95,000 international fee-paying students enrolled with public and private education providers in New Zealand in the 2009 calendar year. Of these, nearly 30,000 were enrolled with public higher education institutions.

- The top five places of origin in 2009 were China and Hong Kong, South Korea, Japan, India and Saudi Arabia.

- There was an overall six percent increase in the number of fee-paying international students during the 2009 calendar year.

- The Code of Practice for the Pastoral Care of International Students is a national-level policy that higher education institutions and other education providers are required to adhere to.

Source: New Zealand Ministry of Education

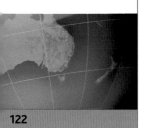

REGION:
Oceania
COUNTRY:
New Zealand

The Ministry funds a small number of Doctoral Research Scholarships for selected international students. The Ministry also validates the requirements for student exchange programs which are run by particular education providers (such as schools and universities).

The Ministry employs a network of education counselors working in New Zealand embassies in particular countries, notably in China, India, Saudi Arabia, the European Union, Malaysia, and Chile. The counselors are responsible for building inter-agency relationships with the education authorities in the country where they are based, and to help promote New Zealand's education system and qualifications structure.

The Ministry of Education collects data on enrollments of international students by course, institution type and nationality, and on the fee revenues earned by education providers. These data are regularly released publicly on the Ministry's statistical website (www.educationcounts.govt.nz) and have been used to form the basis of economic assessments of the value of international education to New Zealand. This information has tended to reinforce government and sector support for the expansion of promotion activities to attract more international students.

REGION: **Middle East and North Africa**

By Raisa Belyavina, Institute of International Education (IIE) and
Adnan El-Amine, Lebanese Association for Educational Studies (LAES)

Mobility within the higher education sphere in the Middle East and North Africa (MENA) has seen rapid growth in recent years; increasing numbers of students from the region are leaving home in pursuit of higher education abroad. For many years, the Middle East has drawn students to a number of flagship higher education institutions within the region, including American University of Beirut and American University of Cairo, which have provided students from the region and around the world the opportunity to study in an international setting. Today, the Middle East is the leading host region of branch campuses of foreign universities, and has seen the opening of new world-class institutions. Educational establishments such as Qatar's Education City, Dubai's Knowledge Village and International Academic City, New York University-Abu Dhabi and Saudi Arabia's King Abdullah University of Science and Technology (KAUST) are attracting students from the region and around the world. According to the Observatory on Borderless Higher Education, there are 162 branch campuses among the world's 15,000 institutions of higher education; over a third of them are located in the MENA region, and a quarter of all are in the United Arab Emirates. However, the attraction of international stu-

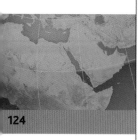

dents to the region is still limited mostly to these cross-border institutions, in which the total enrollment of international students is modest. Elsewhere in the region, only Lebanon and Jordan show high percentages of foreign students (UNESCO, Education For All Global Monitoring Report, 2010).

With the rapid expansion of educational opportunities and the increasing significance of the region in geopolitics and world markets, the Middle East is becoming a more attractive study destination for international students. For example, between 2004 and 2009, the number of students from the United States who received college credit for study abroad in the Middle East rose by more than 200 percent to 3,670 (*Open Doors*, 2010). This trend can be observed in other sending regions as well. In total, the Arab States hosted four percent of the world's globally mobile students in 2008 (UNESCO, 2010). Governments and universities in the region are interested in internationalizing higher education, creating programs and allocating funding to attract a diverse student body. As the most popular study destination in North Africa, Egypt's Ministry of Education has recently announced scholarship funds to draw international students to Egyptian universities.

Approximately three percent of the region's tertiary students study abroad. Outbound mobility rates vary significantly across countries: Djibouti has a 74 percent outbound ratio, while less than one percent of Egyptian students study abroad. The number of students from Bahrain, Kuwait, Qatar and Yemen studying abroad is also on the rise. Western Europe is the top host destination for students from the region, representing just under 60 percent. France attracts large numbers of North African students, who in the last decade have also demonstrated a steady growth in international mobility both within the region as well as to non-traditional destinations including East Asia and Oceania. Students from the Gulf States tend to study in a more diverse group of host destinations, including the U.S., the UK, Australia, Canada, Germany, and more recently, East and Southeast Asia.

The population growth as well as the increasing number of women attending universities throughout the region has resulted in a greater demand for higher education. In the Arab States, over 1.6 million more students were enrolled in tertiary education in 2007 than in 2000. The eight percent increase in the enrollment of women in Arab States during the same time period was the largest global growth of female enrollment rates in tertiary education (Altbach, P. G., Reisberg, L., & Rumbley, L. E., 2009). As more students from the region seek educational opportunities domestically and abroad, national education systems are under pressure to compete with a plethora of universities abroad that seek to recruit top talent. Public, private, and branch-campus universities in the region will need to continue to expand programs to meet the growing demand for tertiary education. Different types of education institutions, such as community colleges, will become critical to meet the diverse educational needs in the Middle East and North Africa. Today, community colleges are well established in Jordan and Qatar is a leading example in introducing the community college model. The Community College of Qatar offers free education for Qataris and will partner with several community colleges in the U.S. to glean insights on best practices in community college education.

While many countries in the Middle East are at the forefront of innovation in the higher education sphere, others are struggling with brain drain and significant other challenges that have hindered progress and continuity of tertiary education. Many scholars in Iraq are living in constant danger, and thousands have fled the country, depleting universities of their most vital human capital. Other nations in the region have limited academic freedom and deep gender and geographic inequalities. These obstacles will need to be overcome to ensure a growing and sustainable international education sphere in the Middle East.

The rapid expansion and diversification of the higher education sector in the region highlights the need for more information on the institutions of the region to enable domestic and international students to make more informed choices, and to allow MENA institutions to position themselves as world-class institutions. One step towards generating this type of data for institutions of the region is a forthcoming study by the Institute of International Education and the Lebanese Association for Educational Studies, supported by the Carnegie Corporation of New York, which will provide more detail on the internationalization of higher education of universities in eight Middle East and North Africa countries, as well as a preliminary classification system that offers data on other key higher education indicators, including course offerings, faculty-student ratio, and qualifications of incoming students.

Note:

Project Atlas is involved in tracking global mobility trends and currently seeks partners in the Middle East and North Africa to provide country-level or regional-level data on academic mobility. International mobility data researchers or country-level organizations interested in becoming a *Project Atlas* partner are invited to join the project.

How International are the World's Institutions?

Key Findings from the IAU 3rd Global Survey

on Internationalization of Higher Education

By Ross Hudson, International Association of Universities (IAU)

Introduction

Internationalization is now perhaps the most important agent of change in higher education. Higher Education Institution (HEI) leaders, faculty members, policy makers and researchers are increasingly interested in internationalization approaches, strategies, benefits, risks and challenges as they look to the future.

The International Association of Universities (IAU)—a global association of more than 620 HEIs and Associations of Universities from 150 countries—has a long standing commitment to further understanding of internationalization, and has regularly undertaken global surveys on internationalization of higher education over the past 10 years. The IAU 3rd Global Survey on Internationalization of Higher Education is the third in this series of surveys, preceded by two others, in 2003 and 2005.

The IAU 3rd Global Survey included two questionnaires that were available in a range of languages, in both on-line and in print format: one for HEIs, and one for National University Associations (NUAs). The institutional questionnaire –some of the results of which, as it relates to institutional commitment to student mobility are presented below—was undertaken in 2009, and drew responses from 745 HEIs in 115 different countries. This represents a substantial increase in both sample size and geographic spread of the respondent institutions, when compared to the IAU 2005 Global Survey.

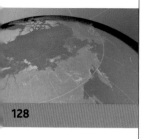

Both the questionnaire for national associations and the institutional questionnaire focused on a wide range of topics relating to investigating and understanding internationalization within HEIs, including the benefits, risks, drivers, barriers, the form and function of internationalization polices and related activities, and quality assurance mechanisms. IAU's 3rd Global Survey report, entitled "Internationalization of Higher Education: Global Trends, Regional Perspectives," provides an in-depth analysis of all the findings of the questionnaire for HEIs at both the aggregate (global) and regional levels. It also includes an analysis of the findings of the NUAs questionnaire and analytical comments on selected institutional findings from HEIs in each of the world regions, written by regional internationalization experts. This chapter will focus on some of the aggregate-level institutional results, relating to an overlapping issue that is also a major aspect of higher education internationalization—student mobility. The chapter begins by detailing some of these findings, and then goes on to analyze what the results show about institutions' commitment to this central issue of internationalization.

Institutional Profile
When analyzing the survey results, it is important to get an understanding of the profile of the HEIs taking part in the questionnaire. For this reason, the survey began by asking HEIs about total student enrollments. Sixty-one percent of the 745 institutions that responded to the survey had less than 10,000 students enrolled. The questionnaire then sought to profile respondent institutions according to the number of international students enrolled. One-third of the HEIs responding indicated that full-time international undergraduate students represented less than one percent of the overall student body, and in 66 percent of responding institutions, international students represented less than five percent of the total number of undergraduates enrolled. Thirty-four percent of the institutions indicated that international students represent less than one percent of all postgraduate students enrolled.

HEIs were also asked whether they offered students an opportunity to study abroad. The results show that outgoing mobility is undertaken by few students. Just under a half of the responding HEIs (48 percent) offered programs to study at foreign institutions to less than one percent of their undergraduate student body, while 28 percent of responding HEIs did so for between one and five percent of their undergraduates. At the post-graduate level, these opportunities are even rarer for students.

Institutional Focus on Internationalization

It has been well documented that internationalization has become increasingly central to HEIs' current and future policy development and planning; this was confirmed by the survey results. A total of 87 percent of HEIs specified that internationalization is mentioned in their institutional mission statement and/or overall strategic plan. Seventy-eight percent of respondents report that over the past three years, internationalization had either "increased" in importance or "substantially increased" in importance to the leadership of their institution.

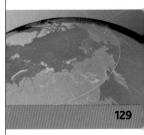

The IAU questionnaire also included questions to understand why HEIs are increasingly focusing on internationalization and what benefits they see in internationalization bringing to their institution. By a large response margin, "improving student preparedness for a globalized/internationalized world" was seen as the most important rationale for focusing on internationalization. This links closely with what HEIs see as the most important benefit of internationalization: "increased international awareness of students."

The extent to which institutions link internationalization with expanding students' international experience and competence is also highlighted in the survey. Sixty-seven percent of the respondents indicated that they have an institution-wide internationalization policy in place, and of those that have a policy, the two activities most frequently identified by HEIs as having a high priority within these policies are, "outgoing mobility opportunities for students (study, internships, etc.)" and "international student exchanges and attracting international students." Furthermore, "outgoing mobility opportunities for students (study, internships, etc.)," was the internationalization activity ranked top as receiving the most attention and resources within responding institutions.

Promoting Student Mobility

With regard to student mobility, there are various ways in which institutions can achieve the stated goals outlined in their internationalization policy. These can include making scholarships available to international students and offering students the opportunity to study abroad as part of their study programs. IAU therefore included questions about these components within the questionnaire, producing some compelling finding.

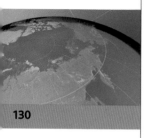

For example, the majority of institutions do offer some scholarships to international students. However, a large proportion of HEIs (39 percent) provide no specific scholarships or incentives to international undergraduate students, and 35 percent of HEIs provide no specific scholarships or incentives to international students at the post-graduate level.

Conjuncture and Disparity

It is apparent that there is a strong correlation between what HEIs see as being the main rationales and benefits of increasing internationalization and what activities are prioritized within their internationalization strategies. Yet there also appears to be a disjuncture in some HEIs between the stated priority activities with regard to student mobility within their internationalization strategies, and what actions are actually being implemented to achieve these goals.

For example, as has been detailed in this report, the results of the survey show that institutions prioritize student mobility and attracting international students in their institutional internationalization strategies. However, the survey results also show that the number of international students enrolled in institutions remains low, and that whilst the majority of institutions did offer scholarships to international students, a large proportion did not; nearly half of respondent institutions only offered an opportunity to study in a foreign institution to less than one percent of their undergraduate students.

One possible explanation for this disparity could be a lack of funding for internationalization activities. Within the questionnaire, respondents were asked what they saw as the main internal and external barriers to increased internationalization within their university. By a substantial margin, "insufficient financial resources" was seen as the most important internal obstacle and "limited public and/or private funding to support internationalization efforts" as the most important external obstacle to increased internationalization. Providing scholarships for international students and developing study abroad programs are both costly activities for institutions to undertake, and it appears that this lack of available funding is precluding HEIs from achieving the student mobility goals that are prioritized in their internationalization strategies.

For HEIs within Europe, another possible explanation for the relative lack of scholarships available at the institutional level for international students is that there are other support programs. For example, the European Union's ERASMUS and Erasmus Mundus Programs and other funds, as well as the absence of tuition fees in several European countries, reduce the need for scholarship schemes on an institutional level.

Conclusion

What is apparent throughout the findings of the IAU 3rd Global survey is that institutions regard internationalization as highly important to both their current and future policy plans. Within institutions, the promotion of student mobility and the internationalization of the student body are seen as a central reason for pursuing internationalization and as a priority activity in the institutional strategy plan. What is also clear is that institutions have somewhat limited success in reaching the goals set out in their policies: mobile students remain a stark minority, likely due to the lack of both institutional and public funding to promote internationalization.

There is, therefore, much progress to be made and also much that is taking place already. This is true when we look at the growing number of national-level internationalization strategies being implemented across the world, as well as regional student mobility programs, including the EU's ERASMUS and Erasmus Mundus schemes. More often than not, these national strategies also prioritize the recruitment of international students and inbound and outbound student mobility. With the current and ongoing global financial crisis reducing public funds for higher education in many parts of the world, the task ahead will likely become even more challenging in the future, and institutions will need to become ever more resourceful and efficient if they are going to meet the priorities outlined in their internationalization strategies, and address the challenges and opportunities that internationalization brings to global higher education.

The report of the IAU 3rd Global Survey on Internationalization of Higher Education, entitled *Internationalization of Higher Education: Global Trends, Regional Perspectives*, is available to purchase from IAU. To order a copy, please contact IAU on iau@iau-aiu.net or visit the IAU website: www.iau-aiu.net.

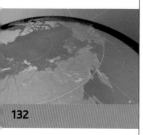

132

OFFICIAL WEBSITES OF PROJECT ATLAS® PARTNER ORGANIZATIONS AND RESEARCH AFFILIATES

Association of Indian Universities (AIU) | www.aiuweb.org

Australian Education International (AEI) | www.aei.gov.au

British Council | www.britishcouncil.org

Canadian Bureau for International Education (CBIE) | www.cbie.ca

CampusFrance | www.campusfrance.org

Center for International Mobility (CIMO), Finland | www.cimo.fi

China Scholarship Council (CSC) | http://en.csc.edu.cn

Education Ireland | www.educationireland.com

German Academic Exchange Service (DAAD) | www.daad.de/de/index.html

Institute of International Education (IIE), U.S. | www.iie.org

International Education Association of South Africa (IEASA) | www.ieasa.studysa.org

Japan Student Services Organization (JASSO) | www.jasso.go.jp/index_e.html

National Association of Universities and Institutions of Higher Education (ANUIES), Mexico | www.anuies.mx

Netherlands Organization for International Cooperation in Higher Education (NUFFIC) | www.nuffic.nl

New Zealand Ministry of Education | www.minedu.govt.nz

Swedish Institute | www.si.se/English

Universidad.es, Spain | www.universidad.es/home_en/lang.en

Center for International Higher Education (CIHE), Boston College | www.bc.edu/research/cihe.html

International Association of Universities (IAU) | www.iau-aiu.net

Organisation for Economic Co-operation and Development (OECD) | www.oecd.org

UNESCO Institute for Statistics (UIS) | www.uis.unesco.org

COUNTRY-SPECIFIC WEB RESOURCES

134

Australia

Australian Education International Official Website | www.aei.gov.au

Overseas Study Portal | www.studyoverseas.gov.au

Canada

The Canadian Bureau for International Education Official Website | www.cbie.ca

Association of Universities and Colleges of Canada (AUCC) | http://www.aucc.ca

China

China Scholarship Council Official Website | http://en.csc.edu.cn

Finland

Centre for International Mobility (CIMO) Official Website | www.cimo.fi

CIMO Survey and Report on degree programs taught in foreign languages in Finnish HEIs | www.haaga-helia.fi/en/services-and-cooperation/alumni/membership/cimo-news/cimo-survey

Resources for prospective international students | www.StudyInFinland.fi

Resources for Finnish students to study abroad | www.Maailmalle.net

Strategy for the Internationalization of Higher Education Institutions in Finland 2009-2015 (Ministry of Education) | www.minedu.fi/export/sites/default/OPM/Julkaisut/2009/liitteet/opm23.pdf?lang=fi

The Academy of Finland | www.aka.fi

Cross-Border University | www.cbu.fi

France

CampusFrance Official Website | www.campusfrance.org; www.campusfrance.org/en; and www.campusfrance.org/en/b-agence/espacedoc.htm

International Student Mobility, Key Figures | http://editions.campusfrance.org/chiffres_cles/brochure_campusfrance_chiffres_cles_n4_09.pdf

La mobilité des étudiants du Maghreb et d'Afrique subsaharienne | http://editions.campusfrance.org/notes/NOTE_CAMPUSFRANCE_17.pdf

CNOUS (Centre national des œuvres universitaires et scolaires) |
www.cnous.fr/index.php?lg=en

Égide | www.egide.asso.fr/jahia/Jahia/lang/en/accueil

Ministry of Higher Education and Research (in French) |
www.enseignementsup-recherche.gouv.fr/pid20155/europe-et-international.html
www.enseignementsup-recherche.gouv.fr/pid20238/la-strategie-en-matiere-de-
cooperation-internationale.html
www.enseignementsup-recherche.gouv.fr/pid20119/mobilite-des-etudiants.html

Ministry of Foreign and European Affairs |
www.diplomatie.gouv.fr/en/espaces_dedies.php3?id_rubrique=2192

Germany

The German Academic Exchange Service (DAAD) Official Website |
http://www.daad.de/de/index.html

DAAD partners within Germany | http://www.daad.de/partner/en/index.html

DAAD program database for foreigners |
http://www.daad.de/deutschland/foerderung/stipendiendatenbank/00462.de.html

DAAD program database for German citizens |
http://www.daad.de/ausland/foerderungsmoeglichkeiten/stipendiendatenbank/0065
8.de.html

DAAD Annual statistical publication on inbound and outbound mobility |
www.wissenschaft-weltoffen.de

India

Association of Indian Universities Official Website | www.aiuweb.org

National Knowledge Commission | http://knowledgecommission.gov.in

University Grants Commission | www.ugc.ac.in

Indo-American Chamber of Commerce | www.iaccindia.com

Emerging Directions in Global Education (EDGE) Forum | www.edgeforum.in

Ireland

Education Ireland Official Website | www.educationireland.com

International Students in Higher Education in Ireland 2010 Report |
http://tinyurl.com/347zk2s

Enterprise Ireland | www.enterprise-ireland.com

National Qualifications Authority | www.nqai.ie

Higher Education Authority | www.hea.ie

Department of Education and Skills | www.education.ie

Japan

Japan Student Services Organization Official Website | www.jasso.go.jp/index_e.html

Ministry of Education, Culture, Sports, Science & Technology (MEXT) | www.mext.go.jp/english

Support Programs for International Students | www.jasso.go.jp/about_jasso/documents/outline09_04.pdf

Joint Statement on the Tenth Anniversary of Trilateral Cooperation among the People's Republic of China, Japan and the Republic of Korea | www.mofa.go.jp/region/asia-paci/jck/meet0910/joint-1.pdf

Mexico

The National Association of Universities and Higher Education Institutions Official Website | www.anuies.mx

National Council for Science and Technology (CONACYT) | www.conacyt.mx/Paginas/default.aspx

Netherlands

Netherlands Organization for International Cooperation in Higher Education Official Website | www.nuffic.nl

Study in Holland Website | www.studyinholland.nl

New Zealand

New Zealand Ministry of Education Official Website | www.minedu.govt.nz

New Zealand Ministry of Education Research, Statistics and Analysis Website | www.educationcounts.govt.nz

Universities New Zealand Website | www.nzvcc.ac.nz

The Education New Zealand Trust | www.educationnz.org.nz

Two recent published articles on the value of international education for New Zealand's economy and diplomatic relationships:

Friends, Foreign and Domestic: (Re)converging New Zealand's Export Education and Foreign Policies by Andrew Butcher. Policy Quarterly, November 2009 | http://ips.ac.nz/publications/files/d6240b4e61f.pdf

International Education and Economic Transformation by Brett Parker. Policy Quarterly, September 2008 | http://ips.ac.nz/publications/files/b00132087ac.pdf

South Africa

International Education Association of South Africa Official Website | www.ieasa.studysa.org

Spain

Fundación Universidad.es Website (in English) |
www.universidad.es/home_en/lang.en

Ministry of Education | www.educacion.es

Universidad 2015 Strategy | www.educacion.es/eu2015

European website | www.ehea.info

Sweden

Swedish Institute Website (in English) | www.si.se/English

International Program Office | www.programkontoret.se

Swedish National Agency for Higher Education | www.hsv.se

STINT—The Foundation for Internationalization of Research | www.stint.se

Ministry of Education | www.sweden.gov.se

United Kingdom

British Council Official Website | www.britishcouncil.org

British Council Learning | www.britishcouncil.org/learning-uk-education-training-
providers

United States

Institute of International Education (IIE) Official Website | www.iie.org

Project Atlas data and mobility statistics for leading host and sending countries |
www.iie.org/projectatlas

Open Doors data and mobility statistics for the U.S. | www.iie.org/opendoors

Center for International Partnerships in Higher Education | www.iie.org/cip

Bureau of Educational and Cultural Affairs (ECA) | http://exchanges.state.gov

EducationUSA | www.educationusa.state.gov

Fulbright Program | http://fulbright.state.gov/ and http://www.iie.org/fulbright

Benjamin A. Gilman International Scholarship | www.iie.org/en/Programs/Gilman-
Scholarship-Program

Boren Scholarships and Fellowships | www.borenawards.org

REFERENCES

Altbach, P. G., Reisberg, L., & Rumbley, L. E. (2009). *Trends in Global Higher Education: Tracking an Academic Revolution; Executive Summary.* Paris, France: United Nations Educational, Scientific and Cultural Organization (UNESCO).

Association of Universities and Colleges of Canada. (2007). *Internationalizing Canadian Campuses.* Ottowa, ON: AUCC.

Bhandari, R. (2010). *International India: A Turning Point in Educational Exchange with the U.S.* New York: Institute of International Education.

Bhandari, R. & Blumenthal, P. (2011). *International Students and Global Mobility in Higher Education: National Trends and New Directions.* New York: Palgrave Macmillan.

Bhandari, R., & Chow, P. (2009). *Open Doors 2009: Report on International Educational Exchange.* New York: Institute of International Education.

Bhandari, R., & Laughlin, S. (2009). *Higher Education on the Move: New Developments in Global Mobility.* New York: Institute of International Education.

Brenn-White, M., & van Rest, E. (Fall 2010). Trends in English-Taught Master's Programs in Europe. *IIE Networker Magazine,* 20-23.

Butcher, A. (2009). Friends, Foreign and Domestic: (Re)converging New Zealand's Export Education and Foreign Policies. *Policy Quarterly, 5*(4), 64-70.

Chow, P. & Bhandari, R. (2010). *Open Doors 2010: Report on International Educational Exchange.* New York: Institute of International Education.

Department of Foreign Affairs and International Trade Canada. (July 2009). *The Economic Impact of International Education in Canada.* Retrieved from http://www.international.gc.ca/education/impact.aspx?lang=eng.

Education Ireland. (2010). *International Students in Ireland in 2009/2010.* Dublin, Ireland: Enterprise Ireland.

Egron-Polak, E., & Hudson, R. (2010). *Internationalization of Higher Education: Global Trends, Regional Perspectives; IAU 3rd Global Survey Report.* Paris, France: International Association of Universities.

Garam, I. (2009). *Vieraskieliset Tutkinto-Ohjelmat Suomalaisissa Korkeakouluissa.* Finland: Kansainvälisen liikkuvuuden ja yhteistyön keskus CIMO.

Greenshields, C. (2009). *Tools and Services You Can Use.* Retrieved from http://www.languagescanada.ca/files/DFAIT%20Presentation%20Calgary%202009.pdf.

Gutierrez, R., Hawthorne, A., Kirk, M., & Powers, C. (Spring 2009). Expanding Education Abroad in the Arab World. *IIE Networker Magazine,* 35-36.

Humphries, J., Knight-Grofe, J., & Klabunde, N. (2009). *Canada First: The 2009 Survey of International Students in Canada.* Ottawa, ON: Canadian Bureau for International Education.

Institute of International Education. (Spring 2009). Princess Ghida Talal of Jordan Receives IIE Humanitarian Award. *IIE Networker Magazine,* 21-22.

International Rescue Committee. (May 20, 2009). *New University-NGO Partnership to Create Center of Excellence for Education in Emergencies in East Africa.* Retrieved from http://www.theirc.org/news/new-university-ngo-partnership-create-center-excellence-education-emergencies-east-africa-media

Kelo, M., Teichler, U., & Wächter, B. (Eds.). (2006). *Eurodata: Student Mobility in European Higher Education*. Bonn, Germany: Lemmens Verlags- & Mediengesellschaft.

Kishun, R. (Fall 2008). Measuring International Student Mobility Trends In and Out of Africa. *IIE Networker Magazine*, 22-26.

Ministère de l'Education nationale/ Ministère de l'Enseignement supérieur et de la Recherche. (2010). *Repères et références statistiques sur les enseignements, la formation et la recherche*. Paris, France: Ministére de l'Education nationale (DEPP).

O'Hara, S. (2010). *Higher Education in Africa: Equity, Access, Opportunity*. New York: Institute of International Education.

Organization for Economic Co-operation and Development. (2008). *Education at a Glance 2008*. Paris: OECD.

Organization for Economic Co-operation and Development. (2010). *Education at a Glance 2010*. Paris: OECD.

Parker, B. (2008). International Education and Economic Transformation. *Policy Quarterly*, *4*(3), 37-43.

Teferra, D. and Knight, J. (Eds.). (2008). *African Higher Education: the International Dimension*. Chestnut Hill, MA: Boston College Center for International Higher Education; Accra, Ghana: Association of African Universities.

United Nations Educational, Scientific and Cultural Organization Institute for Statistics. (2009). *Global Education Digest 2009: Comparing Education Statistics Around the World*. Montreal, Quebec: UNESCO Institute for Statistics.

United Nations Educational, Scientific and Cultural Organization Institute for Statistics. (2010). *Global Education Digest 2010: Comparing Education Statistics Around the World*. Montreal, Quebec: UNESCO Institute for Statistics.

United Nations Educational, Scientific and Cultural Organization. (2010). *Education For All Global Monitoring Report*. Paris: UNESCO.

ABOUT IIE

The Institute of International Education, founded in 1919, is a world leader in the exchange of people and ideas. IIE has a network of 30 offices and representatives worldwide and 1,100 member institutions. In collaboration with governments, corporate and private foundations, and other sponsors, IIE designs and implements programs of study and training for students, educators, young professionals and trainees from all sectors with funding from government and private sources. These programs include the Fulbright and Humphrey Fellowships and the Gilman Scholarships, administered for the U.S. Departments of State, and the Boren Scholarships administered for the National Security Education Program. IIE also provides advising and counseling on international education, and conducts policy research. The IIE Center for International Partnerships in Higher Education (CIP) assists colleges and universities to develop and sustain institutional partnerships with their counterparts around the world and the IIE Center for Higher Education Capacity Development (HECD) offers consulting and training services to build the capacity of public and private sector institutions to develop and manage international scholarship and exchange programs. IIE's publications include the *Open Doors Report on International Educational Exchange*, supported by the Bureau of Educational and Cultural Affairs of the U.S. Department of State, as well as Funding for United States Study; the IIEPassport Study Abroad print and online directories, and the StudyAbroadFunding.org website.

ABOUT *PROJECT ATLAS*

Project Atlas was launched in 2001 with support from the Ford Foundation and is now supported by the Bureau of Educational and Cultural Affairs of the U.S. Department of State and the participating organizations in each country. The goal of this collaborative global project is to share accurate and timely data on student mobility at the higher education level, addressing the need for improved research on academic migration and comparability of mobility data among leading host and sending countries. The project's associated website—the Atlas of Student Mobility—highlights country-level data provided by national academic mobility agencies around the world. This data collection and dissemination project represents an important effort to better understand international student mobility and to examine the broader implications of student migration globally rather than through a narrow national lens.

Visit www.iie.org/projectatlas for mobility data and information on the countries featured in this report or to join *Project Atlas*.